Fish Out of Water

From the perspective of a parent with college-age children, I thank Abby Nye Suddarth for confronting us so boldly with the reality of what Christian students face in the secular world of academia. **Children need to be prepared for this experience —** *or they need to avoid it. This book is a needed wakeup call to a nation with its head in the sand about indoctrination, brainwashing and mind control taking place at America's colleges and universities.*
— **Joseph Farah**
Editor and C.E.O., WorldNetDaily.com

The ancient Greeks differentiated gnosis, theoretical knowledge gained at a distance, from epignosis, knowledge gained through intimate, personal experience. Abby Nye Suddarth's sprightly written account of pressures to conform to anti-Christian thought patterns and lifestyles is particularly valuable because it is wonderfully epignostic. **Written by a thoughtful young lady with fresh classroom experience,** Fish Out of Water **is the perfect gift for a Christian student entering a secular college.**
— **Professor Marvin Olasky**
The University of Texas at Austin (editor-in-chief of WORLD magazine)

Fish Out of Water *is a must read for every parent and every policy maker in America. Abby Nye Suddarth's candid account of the trials and tribulations of a committed Christian trying to make her way on the campus of one of today's modern universities is helpful and hopeful. Knowing what is happening at the academy is helpful and knowing that there are courageous and principled young people like Abby Nye Suddarth gives hope.* **We highly recommend this important first work of one of tomorrow's great Christian writers!"**
— **Congressman Mike Pence and Karen Pence**
Columbus, Indiana

Fish Out of Water

SURVIVING *and* THRIVING AS A
CHRISTIAN *on a* SECULAR CAMPUS

Abby Nye Suddarth

New Leaf Press

A Division of New Leaf Publishing Group

First printing: May 2005
Third printing: May 2013

ISBN: 978-0-89221-621-5
Library of Congress Control Number: 2005925562

Cover by Left Coast Design, Portland, Oregon

Please consider requesting that a copy of this volume be purchased
by your local library system.

Printed in the United States of America

Please visit our website for other great titles:
www.newleafpress.net

For information regarding author interviews,
please contact the publicity department at (870) 438-5288

Acknowledgments

There are many people who helped bring this book into print and I am indebted to all of them. My first thanks goes to New Leaf Press. It's been great working with Tim Dudley, Jim Fletcher, Joe Gies, and Laura Welch. You're wonderful.

A huge thank you to Joseph Farah, editor of *World Net Daily*, talk show host, and author. Where would we be without the kindness of strangers?

I would like to thank my parents, Charlie Nye and Lori Borgman Nye. As journalists, they were the ones who first envisioned this project. "Write that down! Are you taking notes?" A special thanks to my mom because this book would not have been possible without all of her help with rewriting, editing, and researching, not to mention prodding me to write.

I also would like to thank those who took time out of their busy schedules to read the manuscript in its early stages: Keith Ogorek, a great friend and youth pastor; Judy Streeter for good feedback and a keen eye; Rut Etheridge (aka Most Gracious Sir) for reading the manuscript while juggling teaching and seminary plans; Clay and Karen Barnes (a second set of parents) for reading the manuscript while busy raising their own two daughters; Ann Brizzee, long-time family friend; and Paul Gossard, who bounced ideas and helped improve the manuscript along the way.

A special thanks to Marvin Olasky, editor of *World* magazine for taking an interest in my writing and encouraging me. And thank you Sarah Jennings of www.crosswalk.com. Your help has been appreciated.

A warm thanks to the many people who were instrumental in helping me form a Christian world view and think critically — my parents, pastors, Bill and Susie Chapman, and many teachers at Heritage Christian School, especially Mr. Etheridge, my high school Bible teacher who affectionately referred to our class as "seventh period hedonism."

Thanks to the many people who e-mailed their experiences and gave permission to use them in the book.

The resource chapter at the end of the book would not have been possible were it not for many people willing to cull through their libraries and make extensive reading lists. These well-read friends include: Todd Dygert, Ed Runyan, Tom and Judy Streeter, Brian Burnett, Rob Wingerter, Beth Fetters, Scott Biggs, Keith Ogorek, Jay Parks, Jim Spencer, Thad Keener, and Larry Sommers.

While liberalism has spread rampantly throughout the nation's universities, within those institutions there are brave and committed Christian educators who don't waver in their convictions. Thank you for your courage. Specifically, I want to thank the wonderful faculty and staff in the physician assistant program at Butler University. They are the epitome of professionalism. Their encouragement and dedication to education is stellar.

I'm also grateful to the faculty members in other departments who were antagonistic to my beliefs. Their classes weren't particularly enjoyable experiences, but they kept me on my toes. I hope they can say the same about me!

Contents

Introduction 9

1. Welcome Week 15

2. Behind Closed Doors 37

3. We Will Not Tolerate Intolerance 59

4. Fear Factor...77

5. Responding to Tolerance...............................89

6. Pick Your Battles..105

7. The Party Scene 129

8. Posters and Pin-ups....................................145

9. Survive and Thrive......................................157

   Epilogue 179

   Endnotes 189

   Resources...193

Introduction

I thought I was well prepared for college. I had attended a solid college prep high school and was a good student. I was well grounded in a Christian world view and knowledgeable about a host of other world views. I'd sunk my teeth into the basics of orthodox Christianity, the Christian classics, compassionate conservatism, and was good to go. Turns out, I was wrong.

You won't survive as a Christian on a secular campus by simply being well versed on world views and different philosophies of thought. A good background on naturalism, relativism, pantheism, Marxism, communism, nihilism, and existentialism, is certainly desirable, but if you don't know how to handle yourself when you're under attack for being "judgmental" and "intolerant," you can forget about using what you know about the "isms." The most critical defensive play needed on a college campus today is the ability to deflect the labels "judgmental" and "intolerant."

What works in the church no longer works in the culture. It's pointless to reference Bible passages in a group that's never read the Book. Common knowledge regarding biblical terminology, key figures of faith, and the Judeo-Christian ethic is increasingly uncommon.

The first shocker I received when I arrived on campus was Freshman Orientation, which you should know right now is a terrible misnomer. The correct term would be Freshman Indoctrination. Many schools basically hold students hostage for three or four days and attempt to reprogram their brains on matters of moral relativism, tolerance, gay/lesbian/transgendered/whatever rights, postmodernism, New Age spirituality, and savvy substance abuse. And that's all before the first day of classes start.

The shock waves from Freshman Orientation had barely subsided when I received a second jolt. It was an English class where required reading included not Shakespeare or Milton, but essays on why America deserved the terrorist attacks of 9/11, why we should listen to the kid killers at Columbine, and why "under God" should be removed from the Pledge of Allegiance. Other times the professor brought in obscure poetry downloaded from websites that came to him at three in the morning while he was lying in bed. This would be the same professor that scorned the Bible as a book of myths that no true intellectual believes.

I'd expected an uphill climb at a secular university, but what I didn't expect was open hostility and ridicule.

As I relayed these incidents to my parents, their response was always the same, "And for this they charge almost $30,000 a year?" My parents went to college in the '70s. Things were liberal then, but not *this* liberal. They listened to my stories and found much of what was going on hard to believe. At times I found it hard to believe, too. As journalists, they both urged me to take notes, to document what was happening to me, and around me.

In an incredible irony, some of the most aggressive assaults on freedom of thought and freedom of religion today are happening on college campuses, the very institutions once touted as arenas for the free exchange of ideas.

As I experienced egregious situations here and there, I began reading and researching. Others who knew of some of the obstacles I was encountering began funneling articles and clippings my way. I soon found that the things I was experiencing were not uncommon, although they don't often garner much attention beyond the campus walls.

The indoctrination, the hype about tolerance, the selective suppression of free speech, and the singling out of Christians happens frequently. Their stories are told in this book, too. There's a shroud of secrecy that surrounds much of what happens at college. I have taken the liberty of pulling that shroud back and giving the reader an inside look. It is my hope, whether you are a student contemplating college, a parent who is about to launch a son or daughter to college, or someone who graduated years ago, that this book will energize you, encourage you, and above all, cause you to scratch your head and consider what can be done.

This book is unique in that it's not written by someone who went to college 20 years ago. It's written by a college student today. Someone whose classroom experience is fresh. Someone with first-hand accounts of what happens behind closed doors.

This book takes you through orientation, into classrooms with some far-left faculty members, through the dorm halls, and to the party scene. This book also addresses the fear factor that leaves so many Christian students speechless. And perhaps most importantly, this book holds the myth of "tolerance" under the microscope to see exactly what's crawling around in there. You'll also get a glimpse of some of the poster art adorning the hallways, a look at special events colleges sponsor, and some interesting statistics on the party scene.

This book focuses on the downfalls of secular schools. What is happening under the guise of tolerance and diversity is not unique to the college I have attended; the problem is epidemic. By addressing the negative aspects of attending a secular college, I run the risk of painting a tainted picture. I'll be up front in saying there are many good things about an experience at a secular school. It's truly a mixed bag. No school is all good and no school is all bad.

Even though I have encountered unfairness, intolerance, and hostility on campus and in the classroom, I do not regret being where I am. I have grown to love my school. (I almost have as much school spirit as a cheerleader.) I've grown to love my program of study in the health sciences and I enjoy the thrill of finally finding that niche of study that intrigues me. I love my friends and even my profs (just not on test day). My school has a lot to offer: the campus is beautiful, there are a variety of groups to get involved with, fun things to do, and the lure of a prestigious degree. And although I've had run-ins with liberal profs who are intolerant of Christians, I've also had some great experiences with liberal profs. I've even been fortunate enough to have some conservative professors.

I've taken advantage of my college experience, seeking ways to get involved and make new friendships. I've developed a wide range of friends, Christian and non-Christian. I enjoy that opportunity, as it would be rare on a Christian campus. I've learned to cherish my Christian friends and not take them for granted. I've been blessed to be surrounded by Christian girls in my field of study and I realize how unique it is that we gather together to pray before each test. There are ups and downs of going to any secular school. The goal of this book is to highlight the pitfalls in order to help Christian students make well-informed choices before selecting a school, and to help Christian students survive and thrive at secular schools.

This book is for every high school student who believes in God, the reliability of God's Word, and the freedom of religion. It's also for parents, those behind-the-scenes people who usually foot the bulk of the bill. Finally, it's for anyone the least bit curious as to what's happening on the college scene today. This book contains information about college that you don't get from the summer tour guides who have memorized the public relations spiel and are adept at walking backward.

This book will give you a peek behind the ivy-covered walls of the academic buildings and take you inside the classroom. You might be shocked at what you see — parents more so than students, but there are plenty of surprises to go around.

The first part of the book gives you a look at what you can expect on the academic side of things, as well as some tips for being prepared and how to handle yourself. The second half of the book takes a look at the social life on a secular campus and suggestions for navigating through the maze. The book is interspersed with e-mails from friends settling in at other secular campuses as well as from friends who are attending Christian colleges. Their insights, responses, and comparisons are interesting. You will find a "Hindsights" feature at the end of each chapter that contains tips for both surviving and thriving on a "tolerant" campus.

This book also identifies a network of people, resources, websites, and organizations already aware of the battle raging behind the campus walls. They are groups that will come in handy should you choose to stay on a secular campus and need some fortification yourself. You will also find an extensive reading list on subjects relevant to issues on campus, the Christian life, and various fields of study.

My hope is that this book will give prospective students (and their parents) a glimpse into secular campus life that will help them decide if they have what it takes to wade through the muck and the mire, or if it's too far out of their comfort zone. Honestly, that's a dilemma I wrestled with for a long time.

Decades ago I, too, was a Christian on a secular campus. That's hard to believe since I am now a professor in a major Christian seminary. Many of my current students are Christian graduates from secular colleges and universities. Our common bond is in Christ first, but we also share the experiences about which Abby Nye Suddarth writes in Fish Out of Water. *Since secular campus life has become increasingly more hostile toward the exclusivism of the biblical gospel, Christians find themselves in a distinct moral minority in the classroom and dorm.* Fish Out of Water *is not just an exposé. The book will help prepare the Christian student for the clash of cultures and ideologies. It is a survival manual advising students in courses of action to be taken when faced with the unique pressures of secular campus life. Abby recommends memorizing Scripture and learning how to defend one's faith with grace, wisdom, and humor among professors and students who are illiterate when it comes to the Bible. Boldness, grace, and spiritual maturity highlight Abby's personal anecdotes, scriptural instruction, and suggestions for prayer. In addition, an appendix lists practical electronic and print resources guaranteed to provide Christian students with both knowledge and encouragement for their own secular campus odyssey.*

— *William Barrick, Ph.D.*

Welcome Week

As modern philosophers go, Dr. Suess isn't bad. A popular high school graduation gift these days is a book written by the master of rhyme titled, *Oh the Places You'll Go!* The book, a graduation speech Dr. Suess once delivered, begins like this:

> Congratulations!
> Today is your day.
> You're off to Great Places!
> You're off and away!

Dr. Seuss is right. College is just the beginning of the many places you'll go, the beginning of many firsts. College is the first time you're free from the regimented schedule of high school. You begin making more and more decisions for yourself — whether to go to class, or roll over and stay in bed. Whether to wear those jeans for the third day in a row, or do laundry. College is an exciting time, one more open door beckoning you farther down the pathway of life. It's a time when decision-making and responsibilities truly become your own.

> You have brains in your head.
> You have feet in your shoes.
> You can steer yourself
> any direction you choose.
> You're on your own. And you know what you know.
> And YOU are the guy who'll decide where to go.

I was so excited about going to college that I jumped in with both feet. Like Alice in Wonderland, I found myself in a strange and unfamiliar place, but this one was called Welcome Week. I understand that some years ago, Welcome Week used to be when you went to campus to walk your class schedule, buy books at the bookstore, find the good places to study among the library stacks, and meet other students in your dorm. You know the commercial that says, "This is not your father's Oldsmobile"? Well, likewise for Welcome Week. This is not your father's Welcome Week.

These days, on most college campuses, Welcome Week is a not-so-subtle indoctrination into moral relativism. Moral relativism is the belief system that says there is no right or wrong. Right is what's right for you. When followed to its logical end, moral relativism leads to anarchy, but when it's cloaked in skits, games, group activities, mandatory lectures, and free pizza, it passes for freshman fun. Welcome Week is also an initiation into the drinking and partying scene, with ample opportunities for hooking up, which for you moms and dads is slang for a one-night stand. So much for finding out the library hours.

J. Budziszewski, author of *How to Stay Christian in College*, and a faculty member in the government and philosophy departments at the University of Texas, Austin, wrote that his first two years at college were among the most stressful in his life. *Years?* For me, the *first week* of college was the most stressful in my life.

While some regard college as an intellectual adventure, preparation for a career, or a four-year party, Budziszewski said he regarded it as a trial.

"The trial most parents and incoming students don't expect is indoctrination," Budziszewski wrote in a magazine article that I'd read my senior year in high school.[1] After going through Welcome Week, I believe that Budziszewski had put it mildly.

Welcome Week was billed as four days of festivities where students make new friends, build meaningful relationships, and grow oriented to college life. A little fun here, a little fun there, a little fun everywhere.

Events kicked off with all the freshmen milling about on the grassy quad. We swatted away the mosquitoes as the sun cranked up the heat. An upperclassman began yelling instructions into a megaphone. It was an icebreaker, a way to meet new people. Our directions were to spread out and break into groups of three. Each group of three would then interact with other groups of three spread across the quad. Each group was to choose a leader. Our leader was a buff fellow with a generous crop of dark hair. So far, so good.

As our designated leader, his job was to assign a task to each person in the group. For example, he would say, "Go shake the hand of the guy wearing the Abercrombie and Fitch shirt and sunglasses standing by the bench." Once the task was completed, as fast as possible, you were given another silly assignment. We had three minutes to complete a round and then we traded off for position of the leader. The game grew increasingly hectic as we rushed to follow the commands while other people were running across the quad trying to follow their commands.

Fortunately, I ended up in a pretty tame group. We stuck to directives like running up to people and asking for their birth dates, intended major, and what their favorite color was. The game was pretty fun, but as I looked around, I was shocked at what some of the students in the other groups were doing. In the group next to ours, girls were running up to kiss boys they'd never met, guys were doing a vulgar pelvic thrust, and girls stood three inches from the guys, gyrating like Britney Spears.

From there, we moved on to additional icebreakers. We assembled on the grassy quad once again, this time realizing that it would be a good idea to use that SPF30 suntan lotion buried back in the dorm somewhere.

In this new, getting-to-know-you round, the orientation leader gripped a megaphone and shouted a question that everybody answered simultaneously.

"What state are you from?"

"What's your favorite TV show?"

"What's the name of your pet?"

I suppose, theoretically, when you shout that you're from Chicago, your favorite television show is *Friends*, and your dog's name is Spot, you will hear someone 200 people away shout the same thing, seek them out, and build a lasting friendship. Or not. Perhaps it was not intended as a way to meet other people, but to become more self-aware of who we were, and where we came from, as our answers echoed in our ears. I guess it was something along the lines of writing your name in your shorts when you go to camp. It seemed more like something middle school students would do at track and field day, but it was too early to write the whole thing off. After all, it was only day one of Welcome Week.

Later that afternoon, as everyone's energy was draining, we broke into assigned orientation groups of about 20 students. The Welcome Week schedule said attendance at these meetings was mandatory. Here's something I didn't think to question until Welcome Week was over. If Welcome Week is voluntary, how can a meeting be mandatory? A voluntary mandatory meeting? It's a classic oxymoron. Tip No. 1 for Freshman Orientation: If there's not a grade involved, it's probably not mandatory. Being new to the college scene, and being one who was taught to play by the rules, I dutifully attended the "mandatory" meeting.

In the first group I attended, we introduced ourselves, one at a time, and began getting to know each other. These groups have their downfalls, which I'll get to in a minute, but you should also know that these groups are the prime spots where you actually have enough time to connect with other students and form some friendships that will last throughout the year.

Over the next couple of days, we spent a lot of time together in these orientation groups. One of our first group activities was to fill out a little two-page survey.

This orientation leader, another friendly upperclassman, was asked what the survey would be used for. She smiled and said she didn't know. She did know that we didn't have to answer any question that made us uncomfortable. More smiling. We didn't have to put our names on it either.

Oh, but would we please fill in our Social Security numbers? This on a campus that prides itself on rigorous admission requirements. No names, but give us your Social Security number. Hmmm. Would you like a VISA card number, too? Being that I felt a touch uncomfortable giving my Social Security number to . . . wait, that's right, I had no clue to whom I was giving my Social Security number! I left it blank.

I moved on to the questions, which I assumed would be the usual fluff about your intended major, whether you plan to one day attend graduate school, how many hours you plan to study, and the number of beers you plan on drinking on an hourly basis. I poised my pencil, ready to fill in the little bubbles, then did a double take. The first several questions asked for my parents' occupations, level of education, and income. I immediately looked for the bubble that said "nobody's business." Not there. I marked the answer furthest from the truth. I read on. Additional questions asked my religion, my family's religion, whether or not I believed men and women are equal, if my religion believes men and women are equal, if I go to church, how often I go to church, and if abortion should be allowed under any circumstances.

Fish Out of Water

The questionnaire went on to ask if I thought homosexuals should be able to adopt, if homosexuals should have marriage rights, and if I am friends with a person of a different race. It then asked political questions: How do you define yourself? Far right, Republican, neutral, Democrat, or far left? I wondered what my political leanings and how often I attended church had to do with chemistry or physics.

To this day, I have no idea what that survey was for or to whom it went. Maybe they will give it to us again in four years to see if our views have shifted right, left, or stayed the same.

I was willing to put these experiences behind me, as I was looking forward to one of the highlights of Welcome Week, a lecture by well-known author James McBride. At the Spring Orientation session, all of the freshmen and faculty were given a free paperback copy of his *New York Times* best seller book *The Color of Water*. We were told to read it by the start of school. Another mandatory exercise. I was looking forward to this event. I looked forward to an interesting discussion, but of the 20 students in my group, I was the only one who had read the entire book. Perhaps I was more naive than others in understanding the nature of "mandatory." Needless to say, we skipped having a small-group book discussion. We proceeded to the lecture where McBride would be the featured speaker.

The Color of Water is a novel about McBride's mother. She was raised as an Orthodox Jew in the South, abandoned her heritage, moved to Harlem, married a black man, and raised 12 children — all of whom completed college. *The Color of Water* is a loving tribute to a remarkable woman.

Students streamed into the large auditorium in the performing arts center. McBride strode to the podium and began speaking. He seemed an engaging and laid-back fellow who paced the stage and nonchalantly unpacked an interesting discourse. He was talking about the faith of his mother when he casually, yet authoritatively, pronounced all religions the same. At first I wasn't sure I heard him right, but I did. That's right, every religion is the same. I was a little taken back to hear that. As a matter of fact, at the moment McBride made the statement, I thought I felt a slight tremble ripple through the floor of the auditorium. I think it was Martin Luther, John Calvin, Methodists, Muslims, and Jews, all spinning in their graves. McBride is a fine author and the book was a good read, but McBride is to theology what Barbara Streisand is to international politics. With no argument to back it up, McBride equated Allah of Islam with the deity of the Hindus, and the God of Judaism and Christianity. There is no difference among the gods. Absolutely none. Everybody's god is good. And God loves everyone.

No sooner had McBride pronounced all of the world's great religions to be one-size-fits-all, than a noise slowly began building in the auditorium. I thought the low rumble was people about to boo the author off the stage for such unorthodoxy. Then I realized the growing noise was applause, coming from the back, slowly rolling forward, filling the auditorium. Heads were nodding in agreement with McBride. Yes, all gods are the same, all religions are the same. By my calculations, we were only three seconds from our first freshman class group hug.

I was beginning to think that perhaps these getting-to-know-you exercises with a leftward slant weren't isolated. Maybe they were even intended. Could it really be a coincidence that every Welcome Week activity had a strong politically correct undertow?

Putting the activities in the back of my mind, I gathered up some new friends and attempted a real challenge: making slice and bake cookies in the dorm's kitchenette. We used that time to relax, laugh, have fun, and get to know each other. We also went door to door with the cookies in the dorm, introducing ourselves to a few others. (Never underestimate the power of cookies when it comes to networking.)

The next morning we resumed Freshman Orientation. I met up with my orientation group outside the campus Starbucks to go watch some "interactive" skits on college life. I was hoping this would be an entertaining time to relax and laugh, with jokes on dorm life, cafeteria food, and wacky professors. Perhaps the audience would even get pulled into funny stunts as they do on *Whose Line Is It Anyway?* I was wrong.

The first skit portrayed a girl, "Kim," asking a boy, "Mike," what she did at the party last night. Apparently Kim had too much to drink, got drunk, and consented to have sex with Mike. Kim then got mad because this meant Mike raped her. The interactive part came into play when the actors and the skit's narrator invited the audience to ask questions of the characters or to give advice.

Inquiring minds wanted to know: Had Mike slipped a drug into Kim's drink? Did Mike have any STD's? Did Mike use a condom?

Mike revealed that he didn't use any drugs. Kim was the one who wanted to have sex, and it slipped his mind to use a condom. For a minute I thought I was watching an episode of some no-brain teen movie, but I checked the wall and the university seal was still there.

No one questioned the blatant issue of Mike and Kim's underage drinking. None of the questions dealt with the immorality or the emotional and spiritual ramifications of premarital sex. None of the questions dealt with the fallout and consequences of reckless behavior. Nor did anyone ask Kim or Mike if they considered a lifestyle of casual sex to be rewarding and fulfilling. The questions assumed this was normal activity and that everyone in the room condoned it. At this moment, it didn't appear that college was an environment that encouraged freedom *of* thought as much as it encouraged freedom *from* thought.

The next skit dealt with two lesbian lovers who had received an anonymous threatening note. When students asked questions, they asked whether the lesbians had come out of the closet. Would they take the note to the police? When it was revealed that one lesbian was still in the closet, the audience enthusiastically encouraged her to come out of the closet and talk with her family about her sexuality. Again, no one asked whether they thought homosexuality is moral or immoral, or a healthy or unhealthy choice. The lifestyle was accepted without question or reservation, and it was clear that anyone who didn't accept it was a homophobe.

In the final skit, a girl found drugs in her roommate's book bag. The problem with drugs in the backpack was that the roommates had an agreement not to have drugs in the room. While the girl would prefer her roommate not do drugs at all, she can't impose her morality on her roommate, so she just insists she keep the drugs out of the dorm room. The point of the skit was that it is worse to snoop in someone's bag, than to use illegal drugs. Snooping is bad, but illegal drugs are okay as long as you keep them out of the room.

Welcome Week wasn't anything like Spring Orientation. Spring Orientation was a luncheon for parents and students in a large stately hall with huge windows that framed enormous shade trees. It was very upscale, very classy. Even the school mascot, a bulldog, was there in his little blue sweater, barking on cue. The luncheon was preceded with a series of speakers from various campus departments. Each speaker was poised, polished, and highly professional. The college president gave a short inspiring address. Representatives from different departments gave brief presentations, and by the end of Spring Orientation, parents and students alike were thinking this was an intellectual oasis founded on the academic pillars of honesty, integrity, and wisdom.

If Ward and June Cleaver had scripted the lines for Spring Orientation, surely Beavis and Butthead had written the lines for Welcome Week.

A number of the elements of Welcome Week were crazy fun and provided the opportunity to build new friendships. Don't get me wrong, there are some merits to Freshman Orientation — it does help you get your feet on the ground. But — and this is a big but — the indoctrination into moral relativism during Welcome Week was powerful. The message of Welcome Week was unmistakably simple and straightforward:

- You will be part of the group. You will think like the group, act like the group, approve of the group, and agree with the group. No discussion. No disagreement.

- Check your provincial, outdated religious beliefs at the door. We're the ones writing doctrine here.

- Homosexuality is normal, and if you think it isn't, you must be really, really sick.

- Everyone drinks until they puke and has premarital sex at college, so *puhhleese* use a condom!

I had enough of Welcome Week. In a small surge of rebellion, or civil disobedience, I decided to skip out of the last few activities, including an interactive rape seminar. Interactive rape? I decided to pass. As I walked back to my room, exhausted from the indoctrination, the normalization of immorality and, leery of the battle looming ahead, I passed a marker board in the dorm with a message that read: "*Thanks for having sex with me, even though you didn't come to Welcome Week.*"

I crashed on my bed in my dorm room. I stared up at the underside of my roommate's bunk bed above me. I recalled the fun we had had shopping together, picking out our matching comforters, and hanging the goofy yellow and blue star-shaped lights that we'd draped over our closet doors. I remembered the buzz I had the first time I entered the college bookstore, the sight of all those brand new books just waiting for yellow highlighters and notes in the margin. Those feelings of excitement and energy had waned. They were almost gone completely. What I felt now was melancholy and gloom. I studied the pictures of my friends from high school tacked to the bulletin board by my computer and wondered what they were experiencing at the various colleges they had chosen to attend. As a Christian, I had expected in-depth discussions, the free exchange of ideas, and lively debate on issues. I had expected to swim against the tide at a secular college — I just didn't know the current would be so strong.

Was it like this everywhere? I wondered if I was the only one kicking and screaming on the inside at Welcome Week, or if most students swallowed this garbage whole without a second thought. From what I saw, it appeared to be one massive exercise in group think, and the group seemed to be going along quite willingly, if not cheerfully. Frankly, it was depressing. Surely it wasn't like this on every campus. Maybe I'd just picked one of the quirkier colleges in the country.

Several days later I picked up a copy of *World* magazine, the Christian conservative counterpart to *Time* and *Newsweek*. The cover story was "BMOC: Big Mandate on Campus." The story documented how campus after campus grabs hold of freshmen at orientation and won't let go until everyone embraces the same view. The article was reassuring and comforting in a sick sort of way. So I wasn't alone and it wasn't just this campus. I wasn't the only freshman feeling like a fish out of water. It was refreshing to know that someone recognized what was happening, as many of my peers and classmates still seemed completely oblivious.

I bumped into a guy I'd known for a number of years and asked him what he thought of orientation. "How did you like all that PC programming?" I asked. He gave me a funny look and said, "Yeah, Welcome Week was cool. I got like 600 new e-mail addresses." Maybe that was it. Maybe it would help to not absorb what was happening around me. Maybe the key was to be semi-conscious. Wouldn't that be something if the secret to surviving at college was to blunt the thought process?

I sat through a painful number of the Welcome Week activities, noting the lack of critical thought and eager acceptance of everything that was being spoon-fed to the masses. I kept thinking, *You know, this would be a great place to come if you wanted to start a cult.*

World magazine completely agreed. Reporter Lynn Vincent wrote, "Freshman orientation used to be about teaching new students how to find their classes, the cafeteria, and the campus bookstore. But today, left-liberal diversity trainers have found in orientation programs a ready-made crop of captive and impressionable audiences ripe for reeducation on issues of sex, race, and gender. The basic messages: People of color are victims; whites are their tormentors. Homosexuality is normal; abhorring the behavior is bigotry."[2]

As I read on, I realized it could have been worse. I could have been at Amherst College in Massachusetts, where gay and ethnic clubs screened the film *Blue Eyed* for freshmen students. The film was a taped anti-racism workshop conducted by Jane Elliott. Elliott is a $6,000-a-day racial awareness trainer whose shrill, militant, in-your-face style is often compared to Anne Robinson, host of the "Weakest Link."

Alan Charles Kors, history professor at the University of Pennsylvania and co-author of *The Shadow University*, calls freshman orientation programs "Thought Reform 101." In the introduction to their book, Kors and attorney Harvey Silvergate deliver a few blistering lines that succinctly summarize the indoctrination process at work on campuses today.

"It is vital that citizens understand the deeper crisis of our colleges and universities. Contrary to the expectations of most applicants, colleges and universities are not freer than the society at large. Indeed, they are less free, and that diminution is continuing apace. In a nation whose future depends upon an education in freedom, colleges and universities are teaching the values of censorship, self-censorship, and self-righteous abuse of power. Our institutions of higher education greet freshmen not as individuals on the threshold of adulthood, but as embodiments of group identity, largely defined in terms of blood and history, who are to be infantilized at every turn. In a nation whose soul depends upon the values of individual rights and responsibilities, and upon equal justice under law, our students are being educated in so-called group rights and responsibilities, and in double standards to redress partisan definitions of historical wrongs. Universities have become the enemy of a free society, and it is time for the citizens of that society to recognize this scandal of enormous proportions and to hold these institutions to account."[3]

My Welcome Week experience had not been unique. Indoctrination and reeducation films abound throughout the country, as do diversity trainers and racial awareness coaches, most of whom charge several thousand dollars a day for their services.

World also reported that the Milwaukee School of Engineering (MSOE) engages freshmen in a game called "Across the Line." This is a diversity-awareness exercise that made the corporate rounds several years ago, hence proving bad ideas never die — they just find new venues on college campuses. In this game, a facilitator reads a series of statements. When a statement is true about you (you are from a large city, you are white, you come from a two-parent family, your home has electricity and running water) you step forward and leave others behind, proving for all to see how empowered and spoiled rotten you are. "Across the Line" also asks politically sensitive questions on matters of abortion and homosexuality.

World magazine pointed out that not every school includes a heavy-handed diversity segment in freshman orientation. Virginia Tech covers diversity with freshmen using "VT Video," a low-key video with pop-up style captions. The film covers racism and touches on religious stereotypes. One segment even includes a nice-looking, young man saying, "People say Christians don't have any fun." He shrugs and laughs, "I have fun every day."[4] Sadly, it would seem from other reports, however, that Virginia Tech, is the exception, not the rule.

At the University of Maryland, students take University 101 classes, where freshmen are formally "oriented." Among other activities, they take a "privilege walk" much like the "Across the Line" game. They are also told to write their "deepest, darkest secret" on a scrap of paper.

When I was in public school, my parents taught me to never write private personal things in a journal the teacher claims nobody would ever read. If matters are secret and private, why write them down? The essence of private means this is something you do not share, but keep to yourself. Doesn't secret imply not telling?

The point of the college exercise of writing your deepest, darkest secret on paper was to sympathize with and consider how homosexuals feel in deciding whether to tell someone that they're gay.

The shallow exercise didn't even begin to grasp the complexities of a homosexual lifestyle. As a Christian, I am convicted that homosexuality is a sin. But I also recognize the pain, the hurt, and the isolation faced by homosexuals. As Christians, we are called to be compassionate toward all people, homosexuals included.

Part of the key to being "in the world, not of it" is loving your neighbor as yourself. That's basic for a lot of people, Christian or not. It would seem that most colleges think that simply telling students to be civil and respect one another is too challenging. Telling students to respect one another would include everybody, even respecting those who believe the Bible to be a relevant book, not a dusty book of myths. It would also include those with conservative views, and traditional Christian beliefs that question things like homosexuality and abortion. Simply telling students to respect one another also runs the risk of falling too close to the Golden Rule, which is uncomfortably close to moral absolutism. So, instead, schools offer Crossing the Line and writing deep, dark secrets on scraps of paper.

Looking back, I realize I was not at all prepared for Welcome Week. I had my prerequisites completed for admission to the college of pharmacy and health sciences, but I had never taken time to do the homework on Welcome Week and learn what it is really about. Under the mask of fun and games, it is really indoctrination to tolerance and diversity. The message to students is to appreciate all people, but it doesn't take long to see that there is an important clause attached to that phrase: appreciate all people *as long as they agree with us.* Dissenters will not be tolerated.

Having a baptism by fire into Welcome Week, I would approach things differently if I had to do them over again. First of all, I would be much more selective as to which activities I would attend. By no means am I suggesting holing up in your room and locking the door. It may be your instinct to withdraw and hole up in your room, but as a Christian you are called to engage. This may mean you need to stop thinking about yourself and your feelings in order to be able to get out and socialize. You may not be in the mood to mix it up and meet new people, but once you get out there, you'll be glad you did. Whether you are in this environment for a semester, a year, two years, or four years, you might as well make the best of it while you are there. Don't attempt to merely survive; take it further and seek to thrive. James 1:2–4 says, "Consider it pure joy, my brothers, whenever you face trials of many kinds, because you know that the testing of your faith develops perseverance. Perseverance must finish its work so that you may be mature and complete, not lacking anything." Learning how to survive and thrive on a secular campus may not be an easy time in your life, but when you become engaged you will grow, mature, and thrive.

Certain aspects of Welcome Week provide an opportunity to get out and make new friends, connect with people, and have fun. Even so, it is not necessary to go to every "mandatory meeting." Go to the group socials, the hall parties/meetings, and the organized games. Steer clear of activities touting "introduction to" or "a glimpse into" tolerance, diversity, or the like, because chances are that it will not be a fair representation. Even activities that are labeled "interactive" can be misleading. You may be able to ask questions, but no matter how hard you try to get them off track, they will steer away from your comments in an attempt to fulfill their agenda of making all behaviors and all lifestyle choices seem equal.

I would also discourage attending activities about "college life" because more than likely they are a guide for indoctrination on moral relativism, the normalization of homosexuality, or yet another talk on safe sex, which is old hat to most college students.

It is truly difficult to describe the intensity of the indoctrination that accompanies Welcome Week. Several times during my own Welcome Week, I thought of Elian Gonzalez. Elian was the little six-year-old boy who fled Cuba with his mother and 12 other people. When they encountered rough seas, his mother placed him on an inner tube and told him to stay put and that he would be saved. Two days later Elian was found floating three miles from Pompano Beach in the same inner tube his mother had placed him in. Elian was in the custody of his uncle when Immigration and Naturalization Service officers kicked in the door and "rescued" Elian at gunpoint.

Elian would be reunited with his father and grandmother in Cuba. Well, sorta. Actually, Elian was returned to Cuba and sent to a special school. It was a school for re-educating. It was a school that would help reshape the way that Elian thought. It was a school that would teach Elian that the wonders of America weren't really wonderful, that what he thought was real was artificial, that poverty is better than wealth and opportunity, that up is down, down is up, good is bad, and bad is really good.

There were striking moments during Welcome Week when I thought this must be what Elian went through at his special school. It didn't seem like I was at a university, an intellectual institution shaped by the works of Plato, Aristotle, and Shakespeare. It seemed like I was at a school exactly like the one Elian had returned to, not an institution of education, an institution of re-education.

I had gone to college excited about the new beginnings, new academic challenges, and the opportunity to live out my faith as my own. I had gone to college with expectations. I expected students to be mature, professors to be enthusiastic and fair, and course work to be challenging. In retrospect, I probably went to college a tad naive and wearing rose-colored glasses. Perhaps it's only fitting that I now remember my first week at college, Welcome Week, as the time when my rose-colored glasses were knocked off my face and left in pieces among the empty beer cans and cigarette butts. Once again, philosopher Seuss summed up my thoughts:

> You can get so confused that you'll start in to race down
> long wiggled roads at a break-necking pace and grind on

for miles across weirdish wild space, headed, I fear, toward a most useless place.

HINDSIGHT

Looking back, if I'd known what to expect from Welcome Week, it would have softened the jolt. My advice is to go prepared with your eyes and ears open.

Here's a nutshell of what to expect:

- Expect a quick pace to Freshman Orientation.

- Expect a lot of ideas that will challenge moral absolutes.

- Expect that, initially, you won't have a lot of down time to process thoughts.

Don't abandon the notion of privacy.

We live in a Jerry Springer world that applauds people for airing their deepest, darkest, most shameful moments in public. Remind yourself that privacy is your right. The Bible says confess your sins one to another, not confess your sins to an entire college campus. You don't have to reveal personal information that you'd rather keep personal.

Play defense and offense at the same time.

You'll hear ideas that challenge your moral foundation. Pray that your conscience remains sensitive and your mind discerning. It's important to deflect half-truths without growing defensive. Play offense. First Peter 3:15–16 addresses this situation: "Always be prepared to give an answer to everyone who asks you to give the reason for the hope that you have. But do this with gentleness and respect, keeping a clear conscience, so that those who speak maliciously against your good behavior in Christ may be ashamed of their slander."

Even when you're deflecting the half-truths and lies of moral relativism, make sure you're friendly. Reach out to others; introduce yourself to as many people as possible. If an information tent is set up showcasing student groups and campus activities, sign up for every club and activity that interests you. There's no way you can participate in all of them, but you won't learn which ones you can or cannot do or not do until you have a better feel for your course load.

Exercise your options.

On most campuses, students are strongly encouraged to attend and participate in all of the Welcome Week activities, but they truly are optional. Exercise your option to skip a few, particularly the ones that blatantly promote immorality.

Pray for wisdom.

Pray you gain wisdom at college, not just knowledge. There's a difference. Some universities may think they're the same, but they're not. The fear of the Lord is the beginning of wisdom (Prov. 9:10). If you don't have the fear of the Lord, you can only have book intelligence. You'll want something more than facts and figures at the end of four years.

From: "Nate"

To: "Abby"

Being a freshman at Centre College (a small liberal arts school in KY), I'm learning what it's like to be Dorothy realizing she is not in Kansas anymore, as you put it, but for my sake, we'll say I'm more like Toto (seeing that he is a male). Of course, the secular environment did not completely surprise me, having grown up around a private liberal arts college. I had a pretty good idea of what to expect, but it's still been hard.

Being one of the few conservatives on my hall (let alone campus), I've been bombarded with new ideas, lifestyles, and values. I know that I'm here at Centre for a reason, God wanted me here, there's not a doubt in my mind. But with a druggy roommate, a gay hallmate, constant "Bushwhacking" from professors and hallmates, and drunks every which way I turn, I sometimes find myself asking, "Okay, God, I'm here. Now what?" The past two nights I've been reminded that love really is the magic key and that the best thing I can do is show them love, real love.

But at times I want to have a huge impact with visible results. I'm left there loving these people with no recognizable results and it's depressing. But then I'm reminded that God is in control, He changes their hearts, I can't do it alone. Maybe the love I show them will have an impact right away, maybe it will take 30 years, in any case, there's no reason to give up. I can still shower them with love and prayer with the hope that one day they will take notice.

Nate

Fish Out of Water

From: "Mom"

To: "Abby"

Hey, Abby,

Your dad and I have just read the University Parent Guide that's been sitting on top of the microwave for several weeks. I'm sorry to tell you we will not be abiding by some of the recommendations. I don't know if you read it, but "Signs of a good student" says parents should encourage their child to be a student, not an apprentice for a job. The article says parents "should not ask what s/he is going to do after graduation as though real life begins only then." A parent should ask "what s/he is learning to think about, what s/he is reading, what s/he has written. A student, after all, is one who studies, thinks, reads, and writes."

A parent is never to ask about grade point average. Instead, we should ask what ideas have held your attention, caught you by surprise, or taken your breath away. Parents should ask "what s/he does for diversion, how s/he plays, what makes him or her happiest, what s/he finds beautiful. Help your student to discover the quality of his or her mind and the color of his or her imagination — to know himself or herself."

Parents should "encourage their student to study subjects which most engage his or her mind, not what the job market designates as the surest, most lucrative employment."

Apparently, the author thinks parents have money trees growing in his/her backyard if the cost of college and the preparation for the job market is of no concern. As you know, we do not have money trees growing in our backyard, so we are very interested in what you plan on doing after college. We fully anticipate that it will involve that four-letter word known as work.

You should further know, that in total defiance of the Parent Guide, we will be asking about grade point average. We also will not be asking how you play with others. We covered playing with others in preschool. We also will not be helping you discover the color of your imagination. (Who ARE these people?) We also will not be asking what takes your breath away. We are giving you total responsibility for your own breathing. And finally, we will not be using that s/he business. When read aloud it causes one to lisp something terrible.

Study hard, plan for the future, and make good grades.

Love,
Mom (a she)

*Who among the evangelicals
can stand up to the great secular or
naturalistic or atheistic scholars on their own
terms of scholarship and research? Who among
the evangelical scholars is quoted as a normative
source by the greatest secular authorities on
history or philosophy or psychology or sociology
or politics? Does your mode of thinking have the
slightest chance of becoming the dominant mode
of thinking in the great universities of Europe and
America which stamp your entire civilization
with their own spirit and ideas?*

— Habib Malik

Behind Closed Doors

W hen the door closes to the college classroom, there's something of an artificial environment that is created. That sealed classroom is totally disconnected from the real world. I've often wondered if some of the more bizarre antics that go on in the classroom would be less likely to happen if the classroom was beamed onto the computer screens of taxpayers, alumni, and parents who foot the bill for four years.

In one of my classes, the teacher asked how many of us were familiar with the term "B.C.," which, of course, stands for "Before Christ." Everybody looked around with faces that said, "Who wouldn't be?" The general response was, "Huh?" Then she asked if we had grown up with the term "B.C." We were then asked to raise our hands if we had used the term "B.C." Everyone raised a hand. The teacher then told us that the use of B.C. could be offensive, so we should use "C.E.", which stands for Common Era. Everybody looked a little puzzled, but nobody challenged her or ignited any discussion.

Such nonsense almost makes sense in a closed environment where the professor holds the power and students instinctively consider the academic cost of questioning the authority. As a result, ideas that have never been tested or tried by reality have the ability to flourish in a college classroom.

In a fine arts class, a guest professor known for being a post-modernist, lectured for nearly 30 minutes one day on the difference between naked and nude. Nude, he said, is physical. It is when you are without your clothes in the presence of someone else. Nude is when you are in front of someone you love and are entirely comfortable. Naked, he said, is more emotional. Naked is when you are without your clothes and you are alone. He drew a diagram on the board with the word nude on one side and the word naked on the other. At one point he listed the word emotional under nude and then erased it and moved it to under naked. He wasn't just confusing students, he had even confused himself. He talked on and on highlighting the differences between nude and naked and injecting the words with all kinds of meaning and connotations.

You don't approach college strictly as a consumer, but still, I wondered how much that 30 minutes of nonsense about the difference between naked and nude had cost. After class, I went to the dictionary and looked up naked and nude. Naked was defined as "having no clothes on: nude." No mention of being emotional and alone. Nude is defined as "bare, naked, unclothed." No mention of enjoying your lover looking at you. Shocker. That monologue on naked and nude had been an exercise in the deconstruction of language, where the prof arbitrarily assigned his own personal meaning to words.

CREATIONISM AND CLOSED DOORS

Not everything that happens behind closed doors is as fluffy as distinguishing between naked and nude. And not all that happens behind closed doors stays behind closed doors. Consider a Christian student by the name of Micah Spradling. Spradling was in a biology class at Texas Tech. The professor, Michael Dini, began outlining his criteria for any student wanting a recommendation to medical school or a graduate science school. Dini said he would only write recommendations for students who had: earned an A in his class, for students he knew fairly well, and for students who would affirm the theory of evolution. Spradling, like a growing number of scientists, did not believe in evolution. So Spradling rose from his seat, walked out of the classroom, and dropped the class.

The professor may have thought that was the last he had seen of that student, but it wasn't. Not by a long shot. Spradling enrolled at Lubbock Christian University. He received a medical school recommendation from LCU and then returned to Texas Tech with lawyers from Liberty Legal Institute of Texas.

When what was happening in that closed classroom aired in public forums, Professor Dini didn't fare so well. Dini had attempted to practice an egregious form of intolerance within a cloistered classroom. When the doors were flung open, the situation changed and Dini had a change of heart. That often happens when people have attorneys breathing down their necks. Dini no longer requires students to believe in evolution, although he does require that they are able to articulate an understanding of the theory of evolution. "This new policy rightly recognizes that students don't have to give up their religious beliefs to be good doctors or good scientists," said Assistant Attorney General for Civil Rights Ralph F. Boyd Jr. "A state-run university has no business telling students what they should or should not believe in."[1]

Spradling pulled back the curtain and exposed an injustice. He did the right thing. Spradling was in a unique position where he didn't have many options. He could compromise and betray his convictions, or he could take a stand for what he believed in.

CHEM, PHYSICS, AND LITERATURE

For the most part, I found that my hard science classes were cut and dried. The chemistry and physics professors were professional. The material was challenging but well organized. As long as

I paid attention in class and studied, I did well. Ironically, the place I ran into significant problems was in the English department. This seems to be fairly typical, as it is easier to inject personal opinion and subjective values into classes that lend themselves to interpretation. Dinesh D'Souza explains this phenomena in a little book every college freshman should read titled *Letters to a Young Conservative*. D'Souza says because conservatives tend to be practical people — they emphasize what works — they are "usually concentrated in economics or the hard sciences. The reason has to do with the conservative bent toward practicality: equations that add up, theories that can be tested, and so on. By contrast, liberals prefer such fields as sociology and literary criticism because in these areas their theoretical perspective never has to meet the test of reality."[2]

He was right. The most intense challenge I met was in a class titled "The Art of Literature." Course material didn't include Shakespeare, Plato, or Milton, or any of the classics, for that matter. The required materials were two books containing contemporary short stories and essays. Even so, very little class time was spent examining the contents of those books. The professor had his own agenda. More often than not he would pass out articles he had printed off bizarre websites on the Internet for us to read.

The professor was very casual. He usually came to class wearing cuffed jeans and white Reeboks. As best I could tell, his idea of the classics were Dockers and a Polo shirt. He didn't mind if we called him by his first name or his last. He was fond of starting sentences with the word "dude" and often slipped an occasional curse into his discourse. I assumed he did so to let us know he was hip.

On the first day of class, after explaining what the course would be like, he admonished us to be open to changing our views. He said, "Check your ego at the door because we're right and you're wrong." That seemed a pretty bold statement to make. I couldn't help being mildly offended at being told I was wrong before I had even said a word. I held out hope that maybe I was in with a conservative professor. (Some dreams die hard.)

I stayed after class and asked whether he had found himself to be more liberal or more conservative than his students. For a guy that was so adamant about being right, he was somewhat sheepish in answering. He said he felt his students were much more conservative than himself. *This should be interesting*, I thought. *Or awful.* I wasn't sure which, but I had an inkling. Whether he was a liberal or conservative would not be a big deal as long as he possessed intellectual honesty.

Our first assignment in English class was to write an analytical response to our choice of pre-selected essays. Among the topics of the essays we could analyze included pieces on big business (aka corporate terrorism), taking "under God" out of the Pledge, and an essay on why we should sympathize with the murderers at Columbine. Our assigned reading topics were so predictable it became fun to guess which politically correct topic he would introduce each day.

The essay that I chose to analyze for the first assignment was titled "Cutting God in Half," which had been photocopied from *Philosophy Now* magazine and was written by Nicholas Maxwell. In "Cutting God in Half," the author attempted to discredit the Judeo-Christian view of God, saying that a God that is all-powerful and all-loving cannot exist because of bad things in the world. He reasoned that an all-loving God by nature cannot let bad things happen, but since there are bad things in the world, God must not be powerful enough to intervene. Or, God is all-powerful but He allows bad things to happen because He is not all-loving.

An entire class period was devoted to discussing Maxwell's piece. The professor opened up the floor to any comment or question about the article. Although the desks were arranged in a circle to encourage conversation, no one was speaking. It was dodge ball time. Look anywhere but at the professor. Students looked at the floor, out the window, at their watches. I finally spoke up and said that while Maxwell made a good attempt at a compelling essay, there were major flaws in his argument, which led me to draw a different conclusion.

I said that I personally believed that an all-loving, all-knowing, all-powerful God can and *does* exist.

Dodge ball was over. For the next 45 minutes the class zeroed in on me and the statement I had made.

"Religion is a crutch," said a classmate.

"There are no absolutes!" chimed in another.

"Wait," I said. "Saying there are no absolutes is an absolute in itself!"

"People are naturally good," another classmate said.

The comments were coming rapid-fire, and it didn't take long to see that I was standing alone. There may have been other students in the classroom who were people of faith, but if they were there, they were tongue-tied or scared.

"Good people go to heaven," someone said.

"Prove the Bible is true. I shouldn't have to prove it's false," demanded someone else.

I did my best responding. As soon as I responded to one student, another student fired a different question. "Who wrote the Bible? How do you know they were telling the truth?" "The Bible isn't the same because it was written in a different language than we read it in today. The meaning changes with the translation."

It would have been a good discussion, but there wasn't much discussing. It was like a Whack-a-Mole, the carnival game where you whack the mole every time he pops up out of the hole. Classmates were taking turns whacking at me, the strangest mole of all who said she believed in God and believed that God was good.

Someone asked if I believed in the Bible. I said yes. There were shocked faces all around. The professor spoke up and said, "Dude, wait, isn't that the Book with a talking snake and the magic fruit? I'm not going to believe in a Book with a talking snake." He then looked at me and asked if I thought snakes could talk.

"If I looked out the window and saw a snake, sure, I wouldn't assume that it could talk," I said. "But, I can't rule out the possibility that it could, or did, happen through God's enabling. If you do that, you're completely ruling out the metaphysical. Are you prepared to dismiss the existence of the metaphysical plane?"

The professor didn't answer. He just turned his head and waited for the next person to jump into the discussion.

For the first time in the classroom, the class was showing almost as much passion as they did during Welcome Week activities. People were speaking up. The discussion continued — well, if you could call it that. A Canadian student who had previously identified herself as liberal, spoke in defense of denying moral absolutes. She said it was arrogant of me to claim that I, and all other Christians, could know truth. Then she identified herself as a religious person interested in spiritualism.

The student sitting next to me suggested that the Bible was full of inconsistent philosophies, then identified himself as a hedonist. I thought relief was on the horizon when an openly gay student spoke out. He said, "Well . . . class . . . hold on. Let's be nice about this. Listen, Abby probably doesn't really mean what it sounds, to us, like she's saying." I smiled and jumped in to stop him, explaining that I really *did* believe the ideas I was conveying. After being called closed-minded several times, someone spoke up in my defense. It was a female student. She said that the class was being more closed-minded than I was. She was agnostic, and the most civil person in class. She was courteous. I regret that I didn't find her later and thank her for her kindness.

As the class filed out, the professor pulled me aside and asked if I was okay. What an odd question to ask a student who had simply been part of a lively discussion. But it hadn't been a discussion. It had been an attack. I smiled, told him I was fine, and walked out. As I walked back to my dorm room, I replayed what had just happened. I'd held my own. I'd done a decent job at apologetics. I had several excellent high school Bible teachers to thank for that. I'd done better than decent, I'd done well. But if I'd done so well and held my own, why was I crying and why was my entire body shaking like a leaf?

I realized that beneath the hurt I felt from the attack on my personal beliefs was a sharper pain aroused from a startling fact. Those people, little more than strangers to me, desperately needed God, the very being they were so quick to reject. It was hard to sit in class with the knowledge and conviction that God does exist when they insisted on saying He didn't. God not only exists, He created the air we breathe, the water we drink, and every 18 year old filling a seat in that class. I wanted them to see that they were wrong, not for the satisfaction of being right, but so they could move on to a fuller life. I wanted to grab hold of them and say, "You're so wrong! And you're so bullheaded! Open up your mind and listen to this God idea!" But it doesn't work that way. I had to take my cues from God. Obedience to Him would have to overpower my natural feelings and frustrations.

In all honesty, I admit there were days when I didn't care all that much whether my professor ever grasped the truth. There were times when I was so angered and humiliated by him that I would think to myself, *Why should I want this guy in heaven anyway?*

Fortunately, God can soften hard hearts and work through bad attitudes like mine. God placed a nagging ache in my heart for a couple of "unlovable" people throughout the year. Even though I'm not in that English professor's class anymore, I still run across articles and think, *Oh, if only my English professor could read that, then maybe he'd believe.*

Never give up caring for a person, even your adversaries. *Especially* your adversaries. Most people will be more open if you take time to sincerely win their heart before attempting to win their head. Caring for a person doesn't mean being a doormat. And caring for a person should never result in a compromise of God's truth. Committed Christians on secular campuses will quickly learn what it means to be used by God wherever He puts you. For me, it meant an English class where I might have been the only Christian. If God decided it was time to plant some seeds and see some growth, then I would be fortunate to be a small part of the process.

BUT CAN YOU WRITE?

The instructions for our first writing assignment stated that we were to use our "own reasoning, personal experience, and understanding of the topic as you see it." After tossing around different ideas and arguments, I felt confident in my essay. I chose to analyze Maxwell's heretical theories about God. I could have chosen a safer topic, but I had to respond. Maxwell had called God a "co-torturer and co-murderer." My thesis was that Maxwell had structured a flawed argument based on dualism, splitting God into half; one part good guy and one part monster. Even Maxwell himself questioned how to put the two halves of God back together again.

Maybe the outcome wouldn't be as bad as I thought. My roommate, who was in another English class, had already received her first paper back. She had argued an issue from a conservative Christian viewpoint, too. She had received a good grade, although the professor had written on her paper, "I see you have taken the stance of a moral absolutist. Please make an appointment to see me." The professor disagreed with her views, but he sincerely encouraged the free exchange of ideas and was civil. Of course, he was also going to make an attempt to meet with her in order to "re-educate" her.

When my paper refuting Maxwell's blasphemy about God was returned, I was disappointed to see I received a B-. I did appreciate the fact that the professor put a lot of effort into reading my paper. There were 33 handwritten comments on it, a number of them of considerable length. All but one or two of the comments pertained specifically to my beliefs. He circled sentences, underlined phrases, boxed words, and drew little arrows to various comments: Is this accurate? Can you substantiate this claim? Evidence? Evidence? Evidence? If I told you I'm an alien from another planet, would you believe me? Wouldn't you demand evidence? Adam and Eve appear to be mythology. Define "good." Faith: firm belief in something for which there is no proof. Your main source of authority is a book of stories that appear to me (and many other scholars) to be largely intended as myth (fiction).

Maxwell had used words like faith in his essay. He used the words "God" and "good" in his paper. He had cited the God of the Bible as he shredded Him into kitty litter. But I couldn't use the same lexicon. The words were different — meaningless, vague, ambiguous — when they came from the keyboard of a Christian. They had to be substantiated, every phrase documented, and every noun defined.

We had clearly been instructed that it was fine, and even had been encouraged, to use our personal beliefs in order to analyze the essay. This grade and this chicken scratch wasn't about writing, responding to an argument, or constructing a conclusion. This was personal. This was about what he said the first day of class, "Check your ego at the door because we're right and you're wrong."

I tucked my paper under my arm and walked back to my dorm room, once again feeling discouraged, isolated, and defeated. Again, I was wondering why I had chosen to come to a secular campus. I could be on a Christian campus, hearing great speakers, discussing fine points of theology, but I was here with a professor so bent on deconstruction and stripping words of all shared meaning that he wanted me to define the meaning of "good."

LET'S MEET

It's amazing how good a girl can feel after she does her nails. After taking a few moments to regroup and refresh, I picked up the phone and made an appointment to meet with the professor and the head of the English department. I outlined what I wanted to address in the meeting.

The morning of the meeting arrived and I began to waffle. *My professor expects this*, I thought. *He's attacked my views, he has let the class attack my views, he expects me to come out swinging about this paper.* Maybe I'd take him by surprise. Maybe I'd just show up with a cup of coffee, give it to him, say I just dropped by to say hi and leave. I knew a meeting wouldn't change my grade. I didn't want a grade change, I wanted something more valuable than an A. I wanted freedom of speech and freedom of thought. I wanted academic integrity.

Time and again I found myself referring to D'Souza's book *Letters to a Young Conservative.* That little book was a great primer as to what to expect in the secular college environment. It became a second handbook of sorts. D'Souza articulated so much of what was happening around me and put it into perspective.

He even had a handle on my professor. D'Souza splits classical, old-line liberals from new liberals. "The difference between the two groups may be illustrated by their attitudes toward free speech. Classical liberals believe in free speech because they are confident that, in a clash between truth and error, truth will prevail. The left does not believe in free speech. Of course, the leftists are happy to invoke the principle of free speech when one of their own guys is being threatened. Once they are in power, however, leftists are perfectly comfortable with suppressing the views of those they abhor."[3]

D'Souza nailed it. Absolutely nailed it. It was almost like D'Souza had been coming to class with me. There were two types of college professors, he wrote, reflecting on his own college experience: "The first group was made up of old-line liberals; they usually wore jackets and ties and spoke in an elegant, formal tone. Then there were the radicals whose politics were shaped in the 1960s. These professors wore informal clothing, wanted to be addressed by their first names, and used such words as 's---' in class. The radical had their ideological agenda; but at least they were balanced by the old-line liberals, who believed in such things as high academic standards, teaching the classics, and maintaining the basic canons of cility. Now, however, the old-line liberals are gone. . . ."[4]

Maybe not all the old-line liberals were gone. Maybe one would show up in a tweed jacket with elbow patches for the meeting between my professor and myself. I arrived at the conference room where the department head was waiting. My professor showed up a few minutes late, looked at me quizzically and asked, "What's this about?"

I simply said, "My paper."

We sat down at an oval table. I sat next to the department head and my professor sat across from us. I introduced myself, then the department head asked what was going on.

I began by explaining that I was convinced that I had fulfilled the requirements of the assignment in a manner that was focused, cohesive, and concise, yet my paper was graded based on a dislike for my personal ideology, not on content or writing ability. I expressed my understanding that grading English papers is highly subjective, but my professor's personal opinions and intolerance for my opinions obscured his objectivity. I pointed out the amusing irony that my grade was based on a personal dislike for my ideology at a university seeking to build a national reputation for diversity and tolerance. The department head and the professor did not find this funny. Apparently, I was the only one amused.

My professor avoided eye contact, studied the table surface, and furrowed his eyebrows. The department head looked over a copy of my graded paper. He asked what I had a problem with, so I pointed out that the majority of comments criticized my personal ideology and were anecdotal based on the professor's personal ideology.

In my paper I had made a comment that doubt is not a sin; pointing out that God was patient with doubters such as Job, Thomas, and Elijah. The professor's comment said, "I have known more than a few Christians who, as far as I could tell, seemed to look upon doubt as a sin, or at least a character flaw." Since when was truth based on the opinions of my English professor's acquaintances? I also supported one of my points with an example from chemistry, but my professor noted on my paper that his "feeble mind" didn't care for analogies using chemistry. Just because he couldn't follow a basic analogy regarding the makeup of water doesn't mean it loses its validity. A host of other comments followed the same lines. None of the comments were relevant to assessing my essay or writing abilities.

As the department head quietly listened and nodded his head, I went on to explain how there were three comments on my word choice. The most astounding one was where I was told to "define good." I said, this sounds remarkably similar to former President Clinton saying, "It depends on what the meaning of the word is, is." If we can't agree on the word "good" how can I write a paper? How am I to know which words will require a definition, and which words don't? Doesn't the deconstruction of language limit what one can write in an English class?

To define every word and present evidence for every statement would require a three-volume treatise on apologetics, which was not the assignment. We were told to write an analytical response using our world view. We were clearly allowed to write using our beliefs as our foundation, without the added task of substantiating each claim. That is exactly what I did. I analyzed. I responded. I said I believed that my professor didn't really want me to prove my assumptions. The fact is, he doesn't want anyone to hold to any assumption that is not in sync with his own.

The department head was ready to attempt to cover for the professor. He pointed to a sentence I wrote, "God is not evil."

He accusingly asked, "Where did you get that from?"

"The Bible" I answered.

"The Bible doesn't say that."

"Yes, it does."

"Where?"

I offered to get a Bible and show him verses if he was interested. He quickly steered away from that topic, leading me to think he wasn't interested or perhaps the Bible had been banned from the English department. He pointed to another sentence I had written and, as if he had pinpointed the problem that led to my low score, said, "You're making an assumption there."

"Yes, I agree" I said. I asked if that was a problem as the assignment specifically allowed us to use our assumptions.

He stammered a drawn-out, "Well, yes . . ." and then I realized it was because it was a Christian assumption.

I said, "Oh, your point is that I used a traditional Christian assumption? Other people's assumptions are okay, so long as they are not Christian. Please tell me, can I hold to my Christian assumptions when I write for this class?"

No answer. The lack of response (and tolerance) was deafening.

I wondered if we'd be sitting here if I was working from a set of lesbian assumptions, Wiccan assumptions, or even militant Islamic assumptions. Probably not. This is what happens when you stick to the traditional line.

As our conversation progressed, it became apparent that both the department head and my professor knew a lot of "scholars" that view the Bible as a book of myth. I countered that I knew a lot of scholars who believe the Bible is the inspired, inerrant Word of God.

"So," I asked, "do I have to believe the Bible is a book of myth just because you do?"

Again, neither of them said anything. There were a lot more questions at this meeting than answers. An uncomfortable silence lingered. Then, as if to put a final wrap on the meeting, the department head said, "You cannot use the Bible *in academic circles* because it is regarded as a book of myth."

The meeting was over. We were walking out when my professor asked what grade I thought I should have received. I replied that I wasn't there to discuss the grade. I came on principle. "Oh," he said, seeming a little taken aback.

I sincerely had come to the meeting wondering if I would continue to be penalized for my nonconformist thinking. I sincerely wanted to know if the goal of the class was to help us learn how to understand essays, or if the class was simply a way to indoctrinate us so that we would mimic the politically correct crowd. Was the only view truly tolerated in the English department the politically correct view? If that's so, what is "is" and what is "diversity"? Many of my specific questions went unanswered, but the big one was answered loud and clear. Sure, I could continue to hold to a Christian world view, but it would be to my academic detriment, as no "credible" scholar believes that book with the talking snake and the magical fruit.

While it was emotionally draining and stressful to face the intimidation of the professor, make the appointment, feel the impending doom as the day got closer and closer, and actually go through with it, I knew it was the right thing to do. I knew I wasn't the first and I knew I wouldn't be the last. I also knew that in order to have an impact during the meeting and retain respectability, it was imperative to act in a professional manner. As a Christian, it was also imperative to be respectful and loving. I had to keep in mind the student/professor relationship. The professor is in a position of authority and is due respect. When you are disrespectful, whether it's by name-calling, getting angry, being flip, or turning on the tears, it just fuels the stereotype of Christians being fanatical, emotional, or anti-intellectual.

If you find yourself in a situation like this, I would advise role-playing the situation in advance. Grab a close friend or family member and have them let you practice on them. Practice your emotions and reactions in addition to your words. Prepare what you will say and how you will say it.

When all is said and done, you will have a feeling of success. Not quite the full-blown thrill of victory, but you will feel better having engaged rather than having chosen to sit back and ignore the explosions. In addressing evangelicals and the cultural mainstream, Chuck Colson writes, "Some leaders have recently argued that Christians are aliens and can always expect to be persecuted and reviled. So instead of fighting back, we ought to be content in our roles, or just build our churches. This can only lead to passivity and despair. As one friend of mine noted, being a peculiar people needs 'to be set against the fact that we are called to be ambassadors to the world, fully engaged with it, and followers of a faith in which the Incarnation is central . . . retreating to a Christian cul-de-sac is not the proper outworking of what we believe.' I couldn't agree more. Only by contact with the culture can we effectively seek to change it so that the City of Man more consistently resembles the City of God. And if we don't seek to engage and change the culture, the culture inevitably changes us."[5]

I was glad I went to the meeting with the prof and the dean, though not right away. It took time and distance to gain perspective. On paper, the tangible risks may have outweighed the benefits, but truth was worth taking a stand for and faith is always worth defending.

I didn't win any points at that meeting. As a matter of fact, it was possible I'd put a rope around my neck for future writing assignments. The cards were on the table. If it cost me a grade, that was fine. I wasn't particularly happy with the outcome of the meeting, but from the looks on their faces, the department head and the professor weren't particularly happy either.

Considering their scowls, I was probably lucky I got to keep the B-.

HINDSIGHT

Try not to look so surprised.

It's a shock the first time you hear your views scorned in a classroom, yet it shouldn't be, especially on a secular campus. Scripture is clear that this comes with the territory of following Christ. John 15:18–20 says, "If the world hates you, keep in mind that it hated me first. If you belonged to the world, it would love you as its own. As it is, you do not belong to the world, but I have chosen you out of the world. That is why the world hates you. Remember the words I spoke to you: 'No servant is greater than his master.' If they persecuted me, they will persecute you also. . . . They will treat you this way because of my name, for they do not know the One who sent me."

Choose your battles.

You can't and shouldn't respond to every slight, dig, and innuendo about the Christian faith or Christians. But there are times when you should respond. If the professor is approachable, try that route first. Some believe it is wise to have a third party present if you schedule a private meeting. If something is egregiously wrong, make an appointment with the department head. Ask who will be present. Make a list of your points before you go. Stay firm but friendly. They expect belligerence; catch them off guard with kindness.

Pray.

Scripture is clear that we are to love our enemies. "But love your enemies, do good to them, and lend to them without expecting to get anything back" (Luke 6:35). It's easy to love your enemies from a distance, but when an enemy is pacing ten feet from your chair three days a week, it gets a lot harder. Loving your enemies does not come naturally. It comes only by prayer.

Fish Out of Water

From: "Mom"

To: "Abby"

Try to suspend thinking too deeply for right now and stop analyzing things. Just let yourself adapt to the new environment and routine. You need at least six weeks before you decide you really, really hate it! :)

Part of this is the culture shock from having been at a Christian school. I hate to see you hurting, but I really do think this is necessary. I almost feel sorry for some of your high school friends not having the same experience. They moved from comfort zone to comfort zone. Not that you can't move to a comfort zone later, but down the line you will see this was a valuable experience. There are three important things you can be learning right now, not necessarily happy things, but valuable things.

1. What it feels like to be lonely. This makes you appreciate companionship, esp. in a marriage on those days when the relationship may feel less than spectacular. :) It's good to know what loneliness feels like. It will make you compassionate.

2. You're also learning the need for the art of hospitality. To all people — and that includes people you disagree with. Hold your friends close and your enemies closer. That's probably not how Miss Manners would put it, but oh well. I guarantee after this experience you'll have a sixth sense, a radar, for people in a group who are feeling awkward or out of place. You'll go out of your way to make the newcomer, the quiet one in a group, or the odd one left standing alone, feel welcome. That's a lovely grace to possess.

3. How to love your enemies. That's an easy one to give lip service to, but it's something else to actually put it into practice.

That's the best I can do for now. If Dad or I can think of any other bummer forms of encouragement, we'll be sure to send you another e-mail. jk, jk!

We love you and miss having you at home, but we also have every confidence that you're going to milk this experience for all it's worth. You're going to get every ounce possible out of it. You're going to leave a mark. Whether you stay a semester, a year, two years or four, you'll take something away from this and it won't just be that you were weepy!

Love ya,
Mom & Dad

P.S. I just flashed on Mrs. Thiennes, soccer coach, when the girls h.s. team was on the bus at an away game and lightning struck nearby. You girls started screaming and Mrs. Thiennes screamed back: WHERE'S YOUR FAITH, GIRLS? WHERE'S YOUR FAITH?

You've Got Mail

From: "Melissa"

To: "Abby"

Hey sis,

Today in Spanish class we watched clips from a rather pornographic movie. We're doing the whole cultural thing. It was about a Mexican muralist named Diego Rivera and a woman, Frieda. It showed Diego paining a nude portrait of a woman — bare breasts and all. It was very explicit. They began having sex, but Frieda yelled and Diego stopped. Fondling, groping, you name it, it was happening. Then the prof showed a clip of Frieda having sex in a closet with a guy. More nudity. It was very embarrassing, especially in a coed group. We had to write eight phrases about the movie after it was over (we didn't watch the whole thing thank goodness — just clips of it). My partner was a girl who goes to Crusade who was disgusted by it, too. We summarized it by saying Diego was a dirty old man. This movie was graphic and vulgar. So much for Spanish being my favorite class!! It was disappointing that the teacher acted like nothing was out of the ordinary. All the students were snickering and such, but he was just watching!! Could he really be THAT desensitized to not know that the movie was something he SHOULDN'T SHOW in a college classroom!!??

Angered,
Melissa

Fish Out of Water

From: "Brent"

To: "Abby"

I was a senior at the University of North Carolina at Greensboro studying art education. I was in a class called ELC 381, which was basically a class to indoctrinate us into a secular humanist idea of classroom management and curriculum selection. One suggestion put forth to us in our text and by our professor was that we should place a rainbow triangle above the doors of our classrooms to "make homosexual students feel welcome." Never one to shy away from a little controversy, I politely informed the teacher that I couldn't go along with that suggestion. I started out by saying that I would never verbally abuse or be unfair to any student who felt like they were gay, because I don't think that is the way that Christ intended us to treat people. I then informed her that, having said that, I believed that to be a lifestyle which was wrong and which I couldn't condone. I said something to the effect that I would not put a beer can above my classroom door to make students who abuse alcohol feel okay about their sin, so why would I do something like that to show approval of homosexuality?

The professor sort of hemmed and hawed around, and I can't even remember exactly what she replied. However, the shock was, I had several students come up to me after class and thank me for the stand that I took. They said that they were thinking the same thing, but didn't know if they should say anything or not. There was even a bisexual student in the class that seemed to be more interested listening to what I had to say after that. Even the professor, although I don't think I changed her mind, was fairly open to my opinions on that occasion and others. I had other experiences in college which did not go as well because of my faith, but that one stands out in my mind as one which was positive and ended up well.

Brent

From: "Matt"

To: "Abby"

Abby,

How's it going? How's school treating you? Ya know, I was dead set against coming to a Christian university but my parents and a teacher persuaded me to look at Taylor. Taylor has a dinner for prospective students in Indianapolis and they called me up and asked me to go, so we signed up. I sat through the whole meeting and was like this is not a place that I want to go, until the end. They had three T-shirts that they were giving out. Maybe I should not have done this, but I did. I said to God that if I won a T-shirt I would seriously look into going to Taylor. I won the last T-shirt.

This year has been hard because my girlfriend broke up with me. It is so hard not being with her. You base your world, and plan out your future around this person, and then they leave. I was fortunate to talk to my Dean of Students for 40 minutes. He gave me great advice, and told me that his wife broke up with him when they were dating. He listened to me as I told my story, and sympathized with me. He prayed with me, not as my dean, but as my brother in Christ. I was talking to Jace, who is at IU, and he was like, "I don't even know who my dean is, let alone could I go to him about my girlfriend breaking up with me." It is such a blessing to be surrounded with people that love the Lord. I have fallen completely in love with Taylor.

Matt

The
academic
world presents
a particularly difficult
environment for believers. As
one that has spent over 25 years
in academia (as both student and
professor), I know firsthand the pressures,
criticisms, and tribulations it can present to
a Christian. On occasion, I have even known
of professors refusing to give students letters of
reference or other support simply because they
question the professor's humanistic world view. If
you are considering an academic career (or even
just 4 years of undergraduate work), it is important to
understand the environment you are entering.

But, I also know that God is ever faithful. He knows
the great need of our society for Christians in the
academic world, both in science and education.
Many of us have gone before, and we serve as a
living testimony to God's ability to strengthen and
preserve His people. The world of academia
is just one of many frontline battles in the
great spiritual war we all engage in each
day (Eph. 6:12). I would, therefore,
challenge potential students to prepare
themselves (Eph. 6:10– 18) and come
join the battle.

— Kevin L. Anderson, Ph.D.

We Will Not Tolerate
Intolerance

Sticks and stones may break your bones, but to be intolerant at college can render you DOA.

When you are labeled intolerant, people — tolerant people — look down on you. They say you are close-minded. You lose your credibility. You lose your voice. The politically correct worship at the shrine of tolerance. So once you are labeled as intolerant, you become a pariah that wandered in from the enemy camp.

The first time I was called intolerant was in a class discussion when I said something about there being absolutes. A male student raised his voice and said, "'Well, you're just being close-minded. Intolerant." I smiled and calmly denied the accusations.

The truth is, those who claim to be tolerant are anything but tolerant. The "tolerant" like to claim the moral high ground of tolerance, but they are actually intolerant of those *they* claim are intolerant. Sometimes this is overt, other times it is a little more underhanded.

One of the issues we could choose to write about for our final essay in English class was gun control. One of the students brought up this topic for discussion in class. A one-sided discussion followed. Everyone participating in the discussion was anti-gun and in favor of banning handguns. The discussion went on and on with one student after another saying guns are horrible, they kill people, they're not used for protection, and we can make the world a safer place by banning guns. Invariably, one student would finish a rant on guns and then another student would add a comment like, "Yeah, I agree."

This continued with student after student offering statistics without citing sources. As time progressed, the statistics got crazier and crazier. Finally, a student claimed that 70 percent of *all* deaths are due to handguns. Basic logic tells you that statistic is impossible. I'd worked at a nursing home the previous summer. We lost a number of patients and not one of them died from a gunshot wound. When you consider the multiple causes of natural death and car accidents, it becomes comical for someone to claim with a straight face that 70 percent of all deaths are caused by guns. Have these people never read the obituary page?

Thinking it was about time to end the craziness, and having recently read *More Guns, Less Crime* by John Lott, I joined the discussion. I brought up gun control in London. I explained that the ban on handguns in England now makes it three times more likely to be mugged in London than in New York City. I qualified the statistic saying I was not sure I had the right number. I was underestimating, I was pretty sure it was higher. (The chances of being mugged in London are actually *six* times greater than that in New York City.)

Abruptly, the professor cut me off, saying, "Hold on, you've brought me to a good point." He said we should stop so he could explain that when you use statistics you must be "*very* careful." For a moment I was speechless. "What's going on here?" I said. "For the entire class period people have been saying things you agreed with and presenting statistics that were completely off the wall and you didn't comment on a single one of them. The second someone says something you don't agree with, you jump on their statistic." There was an uneasy silence in the class. It was clear that the only views treated with tolerance were the politically correct views and the views that were in line with those of the professor.

Columnist Walter Williams writes, "Universities have become bastions of intolerance. America's liberals are known for their strong advocacy of free speech, including vile speech and speech that assaults precious symbols, such as the U.S. flag and the Bible. Liberals are free speech advocates because it's crucial to their propaganda agenda for control. But liberals have contempt for most freedoms, and once they're running the show, that contempt will extend to free speech."[1]

Williams is right, which is why, once identified as a Christian, you will often find yourself a target. This is the thing about tolerance on campus. It only goes one way, from the liberal to the liberal. Rarely does it go from the liberal to the conservative.

Here's another small, but telling, example: In philosophy class, the professor presented two views for believing in God. If you believe in God, you had to believe one of these two views: either an act is right because God commands it or God commands an act because it is right. Here's the catch. If the first is true then actions are never right or wrong unless commanded, because rightness flows from the command. Therefore, even "bad" commands would be "good" coming from God. If the second is true, then God knows what actions are right or wrong and commands or forbids accordingly. The command depends on God's knowledge of right and wrong. The problem is, as soon as we can gain knowledge of what is right we don't need God. As she explained both of these views, she made it clear that the logical conclusion led to a distorted God; therefore, it was unintelligent to believe in God because neither of these two views worked. Believe in God, ergo, be intellectually stunted.

After class, I realized that there were more than two views. A third view, which I was familiar with, was the correct view that led to logical conclusions and allowed one to believe in a good God. I e-mailed her agreeing that the two views she presented in class were unsound. I then presented a case for the third view and asked for her thoughts. I suggested that rightness or wrongness of something stems not from a command from God but from the character of God. The command flows from and is dependent upon the character. Morality exists as a function of God's character. For example, it's wrong to lie not just because God said don't lie (although the willful transgression of a command from God is wrong), it's wrong to lie because God is truth and falsehood is an affront to His character. God set up the Ten Commandments not because He's aware of what's right, but because He IS what is right.

She responded by saying, "Thanks for your comment. You actually hold the third position in which morality and God are identified as a matter of definition."

I had presented a view that was legitimate, and reminded her of the view, but somehow that view never made it into the lecture in class.

NOR WILL WE TOLERATE INTERVARSITY CHRISTIAN FELLOWSHIP

The list of what will not be tolerated covers topics, people, events, and activities that extend far beyond the classroom. In September 2002, Rutgers University banned InterVarsity Multi-Ethnic Christian Fellowship from using campus facilities and student activity funds because IVCF selects leaders based on religious beliefs. The problem was that one of the InterVarsity beliefs is that homosexuality is incompatible with the teachings of Scripture. InterVarsity had been found intolerant, and intolerance simply cannot be tolerated. Kinda makes your head hurt, doesn't it?

InterVarsity was also charged with violating Rutger's non-discrimination policy. The university policy reads, "membership, benefits, and the election of officers" cannot be "biased on the basis of race, sex, handicap, age, sexual orientation, or political and religious affiliation." The key phrases there were "election of officers" and "sexual orientation." According to Rutger's policy, IV should be open to having a homosexual leader.

Why stop there? Why not force the Black Student Association to have a white skinhead as president? Maybe the Young Democrats could be led by a Young Republican and the Tri Delts could be led by a Fiji member, just to prove everybody is truly tolerant.

The policy, completely intolerant, tried to force Christians to deny their own belief system. Two other similar efforts to drive Christian groups off campus failed at both Tufts University and more recently at the University of North Carolina at Chapel Hill. The InterVarsity group at UNC found itself in hot water identical to that of the IV group at Rutgers.

Homosexual activists, often the most intolerant among those who promote tolerance, take aim at evangelical groups on college campuses across the country, accusing them of discrimination.

ONE WAY

The great irony, and evidence that tolerance is often a one-way street, is that while schools such as the University of North Carolina at Chapel Hill and Rutgers attempt to strip Christian students of their right to assemble and select their own leadership, schools such as the University of Missouri at Kansas City set up a special student lounge and office space for lesbian, gay, bisexual, and transgender students in order to provide a "safe space" where they can hang out and not worry about any form of discrimination or harassment. No matter where you look, tolerance has a very selective nature.

Wesleyan University in Connecticut, known for a homosexual prom and offering a concentration in Queer Studies, may have become the first school in the country to provide housing for students that comprise a unique demographic. Wesleyan provides incoming students the option of "gender-blind" facilities. Student housing has been "reserved for students who do not want to be categorized as one gender or another."

I wonder what the signs say on the restroom doors.

NOR WILL WE TOLERATE EVEN THINKING ABOUT CONSERVATIVE SPEAKERS

During the fall of my sophomore year, author and rebel at large Michael Moore visited our performing arts center. This was before his *Fahrenheit 911* fame. Tickets were advertised weeks in advance. There were posters, e-mails, announcements, and a great deal of hoopla. Moore, author of *Dude, Where's My Country?* and *Stupid White Men*, drew more than 2,100 people to the auditorium. Moore bashed President Bush and told the crowd, "Anytime you have an angry mob of voters, that can't be a bad thing." He encouraged voters to elect a new president in 2004.

Moore also delved into current events, taking a few potshots at Rush Limbaugh, questioning Limbaugh's commitment to harsh drug laws now that he was a drug addict himself. "Jesus would hold His hand out for Rush Limbaugh right now," Moore said. "And darn if I can't find one iota of sympathy for the man." Moore's visit was sponsored by our university's Visiting Writers Series. A number of authors visit the campus and, coincidentally, they are all left of center.

It's not like the campus is totally without diversity. A few weeks later, two other nationally known authors filled the auditorium — Sean Hannity and Ann Coulter. Hannity and Coulter also packed the auditorium, drawing more than 2,100 people, and also were received with wild enthusiasm. Hannity is the author of *Let Freedom Ring: Winning the War of Liberty over Liberalism*, and Coulter is the author of *Treason: Liberal Treachery from the Cold War to the War on Terrorism* and *Slander: Liberal Lies about the American Right*. There were no announcements, advertisements for tickets, or student e-mail about Hannity and Coulter, however. But then, Hannity and Coulter were not guests of the university. A news talk radio station had sponsored their visit. The radio station and a dozen other local businesses had rented the performance hall for the authors' appearance. It's not like conservatives don't make it to campus, they just don't make it there as guests of the university.

The local paper featured a picture and story about Michael Moore's appearance on the cover of the City and State section the day following Moore's visit, but somehow the paper altogether missed the Hannity and Coulter event.

During my junior year, the College Republicans invited David Horowitz, president of the Center for the Study of Popular Culture, to speak on campus on April 6, 2005. As Horowitz began his lecture, he was hit with a cream pie. Members of the group that assaulted Horowitz ran out of the room and were chased by Horowitz supporters. The attackers also yelled racial epithets at an African-American attending the event. Horowitz supporters caught the assailants and confronted them; however, the assailants then got away.

I wasn't able to attend the lecture, but I spoke with my friend Carl Heck, who witnessed the fiasco. Heck, who is state chairman of the Indiana Federation of College Republicans, said this was not just a "pie-throwing incident," but a hate crime.

Heck says while ideologues of diversity and tolerance are constantly promoted on campus, neither of them were apparent the night Horowitz came to town. Heck said, "If the ideas presented are not what they [dissenters] agree with, then they try to silence them." Hence, we get pie throwing. Heck commended Horowitz for his response, saying he did an "admirable job." If Horowitz had stopped the lecture and left the auditorium, as one professor suggested he do, the pie-throwers would have gotten what they wanted.

The next day, the university president sent out an e-mail rebuking the students for their behavior. I echo Heck's response to this: "Talk is cheap." Actions speak louder than words, and we have yet to see conservative speakers brought to campus, funded by the university. Yet, the university pays big bucks to bring in liberals all the time. Where is this intellectual diversity that is talked about?

Heck points out that the students on our campus tend to be on the conservative side, but because so many of the faculty and administration are "so out of whack" (aka liberal), it will be hard to foster any change.

Diversity can be a tricky thing.

Giving the cold shoulder to conservative speakers was outright at Arizona State University. There was nothing implied or subtle, no oversight by virtue of no invitation. Here's what happened: A conservative student did the unthinkable — dared to suggest inviting conservative speakers to campus.

Shanna Bowman was vice president of activities for the ASU student government. She and her chief of staff, Oubai Shahbandar, had the audacity to invite some speakers to campus that hold beliefs outside the mainstream of the Young Democrats, Democratic Socialists, the ASU chapter of the ACLU, Minority Coalitions, Lesbian/Gay/Bisexual/Transgendered/Questioning, Lambda League, Asian Coalition, American Indian Coalition, and El Concillo.

For merely attempting to invite conservative speakers that would balance the many liberal speakers who had been invited to campus, opposing student groups tried to have Bowman impeached.[2] The grounds for impeachment? Well, it wasn't anything that she *had* done, but something she *might possibly* do in the future. They tried to impeach Bowman for possibly accepting future gifts from Young America's Foundation, including a "free trip to California" to visit the Reagan ranch. Bowman had not accepted such a gift, but some thought she might, maybe, possibly, do so in the future. Therefore, impeachment was the only sensible course of action. The impeachment failed.

Bowman said she would probably stay at the ASU campus. Her friend and colleague Oubai Shahbandar may not. (Of course, this would all be fortunate or unfortunate, depending on whether one believes staying on a politically correct campus is good fortune or bad.)

Shahbandar dug himself a politically incorrect hole when, as a student senator, he introduced a bill condemning the university for taking down American flags one week after the September 11 terrorist attacks. The university feared that the symbol — the American flag — could offend international students and promote a "hostile environment."

Problems continued when someone apparently hacked into Shahbandar's e-mail account and sent a threatening message to a student senator who tried to impeach Bowman. Shahbandar denies sending the message and has six witnesses who have signed affidavits that they were with him at the time the e-mail was sent. Shahbandar was taping a radio interview at the time and has a videotape of the interview itself. Despite the evidence, ASU had police escort Shahbandar off campus half an hour before he was to take a philosophy midterm exam. He was given an interim suspension and faces expulsion pending an investigation. He also received an F for the midterm, and the class, since he failed to take the exam.

Here comes a delicious irony. Shahbandar is of Arab descent. He told NewsMax.com, "As an American Arab, I have never felt as persecuted in a post-9/11 world as I do now at the hands of the leftist university administration."[3]

Stories like that generate one of two reactions. They either make your blood boil or make you want to run and cower in a corner. Unfortunately, a lot of Christian students cower in the corner. Not all though. Certainly not conservative columnist Igor Birman.

Birman writes, or wrote rather, for the University of California-Davis student newspaper, the *California Aggie*. Birman was the paper's only conservative columnist. He wrote a column titled "The Right Stuff," often expressing strong support for the war on terror and rousing debate on issues from the Israeli-Palestinian crisis to reparations for slavery. Birman was fired from his position on January 1, 2003, even though his contract ran through June 2003. He was fired by Fitzgerald Vo, who cited Birman's "tendency to enrage members of the opposing causes." Imagine that, a newspaper columnist rattling the cages of those with opposing views. What will they think of next? A First Amendment?

Birman recounted his experience as an immigrant and told a reporter, "When my family and I fled the former Soviet Union a decade ago, we left behind a nation where laws were systematically ignored and persecution ruled. In silencing the voice of dissent at the *Aggie*, Mr. Vo has committed the same kind of assault against the freedom of thought that my family would have faced in the USSR for speaking out against communism."[4]

Birman filed a small claims lawsuit in attempt to recover the wages he would have earned had his contract continued, as well as court costs and legal fees. Birman said any additional monies he may win will be donated to the Young Conservatives Foundation "so that conservative thought is given an opportunity to grow in this climate of general hostility."

A CONSERVATIVE SPEAKER SLIPS IN — AND IS NOT TOLERATED

At Georgetown University, a Jesuit university, the invited commencement speaker of May 17, 2003, was Francis Cardinal Arinze, head of the Vatican Congregation for Divine Worship and Discipline of the Sacraments. Arinze is known as an expert on Christian-Muslim relations and is a popular speaker in the United States. It makes sense that a Catholic school would invite a Catholic speaker who takes Catholicism seriously. Or does it? Arinze delivered a commencement address that so angered faculty members that one "postmodern" faculty member left the stage while Arinze was still speaking. About 70 other faculty members later signed a protest letter delivered to the dean of Arts and Sciences.

What was it that Arinze said that so angered the faculty of this Jesuit school? Arinze, from Nigeria, told the class of 2003 that "true happiness does not consist in the accumulation of goods: money, cars, houses. Nor is it to be found in pleasure seeking: eating, drinking, sex."[5]

Arinze said that "happiness is attained by achieving the purpose of our earthly existence. . . . My religion guides and helps me towards this." So far, so good. But then Arinze went on to tell the audience that in many parts of the world "the family is under siege. It is opposed by an anti-life mentality as is seen in contraception, abortion, infanticide, and euthanasia. It is scorned and banalized by pornography, desecrated by fornication and adultery, mocked by homosexuality, sabotaged by irregular unions and cut in two by divorce."[6]

As James Hitchcock wrote on the Women for Faith and Family website, "At that, Georgetown's roof caved in." Despite the location being a Catholic school, the traditional Catholic message didn't go over well. At least not with the faculty. Tommaso Astarita, a professor of history, called the cardinal's message "wildly inappropriate."

The end result of the cardinal delivering a very pro-family, pro-faith message at a Catholic school? The dean of Arts and Sciences publicly apologized for the cardinal's remarks. Clearly, the cardinal's remarks on faith, family, and sanctity of life could not be tolerated.

WE WILL NOT TOLERATE PRAYER

At the Virginia Military Institute, a school where military science is the specialty, students have long offered a brief dinner prayer. The prayer usually lasts about 20 seconds and typically ends, "Now O God, we receive this food and share this meal together with thanksgiving. Amen." There is no mention of any specific deity and no cadet is required to recite the prayer or bow his or her head. The dinner prayer had been a tradition for 162 years and now the prayer is no more.

A federal appeals court ruled in 2003 that the prayer was unconstitutional because it offended several cadets. John W. Whitehead, writing about the case, says, "The military is a special society, and prayer has been a mainstay of the American soldier since 1774, when the first prayer book was issued to members of the Continental Army. And not less than 67 different prayer books have been adopted by branches of the American armed forces over a 225-year period."

Whitehead continues, "This, of course, brings us to the compelling reason for military prayer, which stems from the old axiom that there are no real atheists in foxholes. Men do not generally die for their country or for their buddies. They enter the heat of battle believing that, if they are fatally felled by a bullet, there is something beyond our chaotic and violent world. And many die with a prayer on their lips."[7]

They may die with a prayer on their lips, but at VMI they can no longer have dinner with a prayer on their lips.

Judge J. Harvie Wilkinson III wrote in dissent to the appeals court decision, "The supper prayer at Virginia Military Institute is the most benign form of religious observance. I doubt that cadets who are deemed ready to vote, to fight for our country, and to die for our freedoms, are so impressionable that they will be coerced by a brief, nonsectarian supper prayer."[8]

WE WILL NOT TOLERATE THEOLOGY MAJORS

At times, intolerance has even focused its laser on specific majors found to be intolerable. Teresa Baker received nearly $4,000 in state scholarship money and was promised $2,750 for her junior year at Ave Maria College. When Becker declared her major as theology, the money dried up. State officials wrote her, saying Michigan law states "students enrolled in a course of study leading to a degree in theology, divinity, or religious education are not eligible to receive an award." Accordingly, "your award has changed from $2,750 to $0.00."

Becker sued the state of Michigan and in August 2003 a federal judged issued a ruling in her favor, stating that Michigan had "probably" engaged in religious discrimination. State officials were ordered to put her scholarship money in escrow.

Chuck Colson, writing for www.breakpoint.org called the case a travesty. "Litigation shouldn't be required for students of theology to be treated the same as other students. Nobody claims that theology isn't a serious academic discipline, especially in an age when students can "study" sitcoms and even pornographic films for credit. This case is entirely about anti-religious bias."[9]

FURTHERMORE, WE WILL NOT TOLERATE COOKIES

For those continually looking for ways to enforce their mythical and hypocritical version of tolerance, nothing is more offensive to them than a sense of humor. Those with the audacity to use humor or parody are categorically not funny. Very not funny.

In late 2002 and early 2003 a new genre of fundraising began popping up on campuses around the country — affirmative action bake sales. The bake sale to gain the most publicity was one hosted by Bruin Republicans at UCLA.

Students sold cookies at different prices depending on the buyer's race and gender. Black, Latino, and American Indian females were charged 25 cents for cookies that cost minority males 50 cents. White females were charged $1, while white males and all Asian-Americans were charged $2. The bake sale brought cries of outrage from a top California Democrat and student groups on campus. President of the Bruin Republicans Andrew Jones said the intent of the sale was to "bring the issue (of affirmative action) down to everyday terms. We wanted to show how affirmative action is racial division, not racial reconciliation."[10]

NOR WILL WE TOLERATE MISS AMERICA

One morning, I was contemplating the totalitarian effect of a secular college education when I picked up the newspaper and realized that it wasn't just college. Even Miss America was being dogged by the politically correct. Miss America! This is usually the smile pretty, look good in a swimsuit, and I-wish-for-world-peace scholarship competition. (I learned not to call them beauty pageants from watching Sandra Bullock in *Miss Congeniality*.) But now they were even trying to muzzle Miss America 2003, Erika Harold.

Harold told a *Washington Times* reporter that pageant officials had ordered her not to talk publicly about sexual abstinence, a cause she had advocated to teenage girls in Illinois. Harold may be pretty in pink, but she wasn't going to go along quietly. All of which made me want to add a diamond to her tiara.

"I will not be bullied," Harold said at a National Press Club press conference, as officials tried to prevent reporters from asking questions about her abstinence message. Pageant officials had told Harold to talk only about the issue of youth-violence prevention and to say nothing about sexual abstinence or her pro-chastity message which she had delivered to some 14,000 young people by the time she won the Miss Illinois crown. (An interesting contrast is that Miss America 1998, Kate Shindle, had an AIDS prevention platform and advocated publicly funded condom distribution in public schools and government-funded needle exchanges for drug users.) Harold had delivered pro-chastity messages as part of Project Reality, a Chicago-based group that has been a pioneer in the field of abstinence education and had won the Miss Illinois crown on a platform of "Teenage Sexual Abstinence: Respect Yourself, Protect Yourself." Later, state pageant officials selected "teen violence prevention" as her Miss America contest platform saying that it was more "pertinent."

When Harold attempted to share her pro-abstinence message, she was bullied by pageant officials. Harold announced she would not be bullied. When talking to *Washington Times* reporter George Archibald, she described the bullying she and her family endured because of her interracial heritage. Harold is of black and American Indian heritage. When she was a ninth-grader in Urbana, Illinois, someone once hurled a carton of eggs through her bedroom window and smeared the window with butter and cheese. Another time the power in her house was short-circuited by the bullies. In her math class at school, she said a teacher watched and did nothing as a student sang "a horribly degrading song with words that I am not going to repeat today. The students retaliated in a very frightening way and discussed plans to pool their lunch money together to buy a rifle to kill me. And when I went to tell the principal this, his only remark to me was, 'If you'd only be more submissive like the other girls, this wouldn't happen to you.' "[11]

Harold was not submissive as a ninth-grader and she was not submissive as Miss America 2003. After intense discussion with pageant officials it was agreed Harold could include her pro-abstinence message as part of her youth-violence prevention platform.

HINDSIGHT

Yes, they're calling you.

Anyone who believes in moral absolutes and engages in classroom discussions will be called intolerant. Be prepared for this to sting. It will. Be prepared to feel embarrassed. You will. But once the sting and blush have subsided, congratulate yourself. You have just entered the culturally relevant arena of ideas.

Point out the intolerance.

When you are called intolerant, immediately point out the tangled logic. "If I'm intolerant, and you're intolerant of my intolerance, doesn't that make you intolerant?" This may lead to a tension headache and sound humorous, but it's really not. Intolerance is costing students across the country grades, scholarship monies, and civil liberties. The tolerance police are aggressive and punitive, which is why it is important to speak up and point out the hypocrisy.

Point out that Christianity is truly tolerant.

There is also a dynamic of Christianity that is very tolerant. Christianity may be one of the most tolerant religions in the world. Christ accepts men and women in whatever moral and spiritual state they are in.

Broadsided by intolerance.

Intolerance is by no means limited to college campuses. It is sweeping the country as the measuring stick of the politically correct.

Take a lesson from the former Miss America.

Refuse to be bullied. Refuse to be silent. Stick by your convictions, respectfully, but stick to them. You will have the reward of being true to your beliefs. Sorry, no tiara.

From: "Andy"

To: "Abby"

Abby,

I have mixed feelings about your take on college. On the one hand I feel bad that you don't exactly love it there, but on the other hand it sounds like you have a very clear idea about why God put you there. And even though I was joking about the marriage thing, I still would wager that there are some good Christian guys on your campus. And remember, some denominations are now accepting homosexuals in their churches — so if all else fails, try to convert one.

You asked how school was here. Wow. If one word could encapsulate all that I fell about college life in general, that would be it. There is so much new . . . everything: new friends, new home, new material in class, new food, new activities, new bed sheets. It seems almost overwhelming. The campus has a radiant spiritual atmosphere. Christians in all my classes and all of them very friendly. But one glaring fault of having all Christians in every class is that there is very little challenge to live out your faith. It's very similar to our Christian high school, except there are very few rules.

Another advantage of going to a small school is the tradition and ability to goof around. Last night, my floor, the Penthouse, the most elite floor on campus in the nicest dorm on campus, walked across the commons to our sister floor in English dorm. When we arrived we sang an adapted version of Hootie and the Blowfish's "Only Want to Be with You." I played the clarinet along with two guitars and a saxophone. And as part of this annual tradition, we were all wearing homemade togas.

In spite of the kidding, I applaud you for not lowering your standards to fit those around you. If you continue to be a light for Jesus Christ in the midst of our darkness, surely something good will come of it.

It is always, at anytime, good to talk to you.

Andy

Secular universities are the great marketplaces of ideas. What one hopes for in a marketplace is that the consumers will be able to make decisions about what they want to buy or sell in complete freedom. Likewise, in the best possible world, college students should be able to share opinions and critically analyze intellectual positions without experiencing any sort of intolerance or ridicule. Sadly, that is often not the case. I have heard many stories of Christian students being singled out in a negative fashion by fellow students or instructors for their viewpoints — viewpoints shaped by their faith life. Too often, the intellectual and moral playing field on the university campus is not level and Christian students are at a disadvantage.

Abby Nye Suddarth shares many of these same experiences in Fish Out of Water. She gives us a candid look at the challenge of being a Christian university student on a secular campus and offers strategies for not just coping but redeeming the trials facing students of faith inside and outside of the classroom. We tell our students that they are missionaries to their secular campus. You will benefit from reading this firsthand account by one such missionary.

— Dr. Ben Gates
Campus Minister and History Professor
Indiana University-Purdue University,
Fort Wayne

Fear Factor

The best part about my freshman year in college was my roommate. She was a fellow Christian and it was comforting knowing I could come back to my room after class and share my struggles with her. She could understand why I was so upset. She helped me gain perspective and showed me I was not the only Christian and conservative on campus, even though it felt like it at times.

As we would walk to our separate classes together, she encouraged me, confirming we knew the truth, that our ideas were valid, and that we were responsible to present the whole picture. Those days really made a difference before I walked into English class. I could hold my head higher. It would be difficult to overstate the importance of a solid, grounded Christian friend. Fortunately for my roommate, she didn't seem to have drawn a class schedule featuring some of the far-left academia nuts I was encountering. But she didn't escape completely.

As my roommate sat in freshman biology class the first week of school, the professor paced across the front of the class, turned and asked if anyone did not believe in evolution. If they did not, would they please raise their hands? My Christian roommate and another student both raised their hands.

At a secular school, it certainly would be plausible that the majority of students adhere to the evolution theory. But it is even more plausible that there were other students who didn't believe, or at least questioned some of the holes in the evolution theory, but were too scared to identify themselves. The two who did raise their hands became easy targets the rest of the semester.

My roommate wasn't intimidated and stood up for her convictions with that small gesture of raising her hand. With that simple act, she acknowledged that truth is more important than conformity. There were probably others in her class who thought the way she did, but they were too scared and intimidated to identify themselves. It's easy to be bullied into silence. It happens a lot — even to mature Christians.

An example of how silence can engulf members of an audience happened during the Iraq War. At an anti-war "teach-in," a Columbia University professor, Nicholas DeGenova, told an audience that he would like to see "a million Mogadishus." He was referring to the Somalia incident in which 18 American soldiers were ambushed and killed in 1993, their corpses dragged through the streets to the cheers and jeers of crowds. DeGenova, assistant professor of anthropology and Latino studies, also said, "The only true heroes are those who find ways that help defeat the U.S. military."[1]

The crowd listening to DeGenova nearly filled Columbia University's Low Library. And the crowd was silent. If there were students who disagreed with DeGenova's murderous comment, their voices were not heard. How is it possible in a crowd that size that not one person was utterly repulsed by DeGenova's wish for a million Mogadishus? How can that be possible?

How? Fear. There probably were at least a few who disagreed with DeGenova, but they were afraid to be heard. Fear is a powerful intimidator.

That fear of being the loner in a crowd, whether it's in a campus library or a classroom discussion, is nearly palpable. When the conversation slants markedly to the left and you realize you may be the only one leaning right, fear can be nearly paralyzing. Your heart quickens, you feel flushed, and you desperately hope there is just one other person in the room who will side with you. The fear grows so thick you can almost see it and smell it.

What's to fear? Plenty. The first thing to fear is a grade. I always wonder if speaking up is going to cost me academically. Does the professor have an appetite for vengeance? What will the cost be? A quiz grade, an unfair take on an essay question? Will speaking up mean a lower grade for the semester? How battered do I want my GPA to be? And to be quite honest, and borderline opportunistic, the chances I'm going to change a professor's mind are probably zero to none, so is it worth the risk?

I also fear a certain amount of rejection among my peers. My fellow classmates may hear what I have to say and unfairly label me close-minded, a bigot, intolerant, or a homophobe.

A good deal of fear is generated by the professor because of his or her position of authority. The professor always has the upper hand — more experience, more wisdom, more letters behind the last name. The professor rules the class. If professors want to eat you for lunch, they can. They write the menu.

In my freshman English class, the professor liked controversy. But since most of the students would either agree with him, or didn't care to speak out, I became the one who most often held the opposing view. Contrary and argumentative — front row, second seat from the wall. The professor would present a typical left-wing, anti-Christian, I-hate-America topic in class, give his opinion on it, then pause to see if anyone would speak up. He would try to make eye contact with a student and frequently find that no one wanted to debate him. He'd then look at me to see if I would oblige. Evidently we'd developed something of a routine. Even if I didn't want to engage in a debate, it somehow became a responsibility, sort of like an unwritten job description.

By being called on repeatedly, this fear began to diminish somewhat, but there were still times when being singled out grew wearisome.

My friend Angela was singled out in her speech class when she gave a speech on guns. Her position was conservative, in defense of gun ownership and the Second Amendment. During the in-class student evaluations, her classmates ripped her apart for, what they considered, her nutcase views. Student after student criticized her stance on the topic. Being a target can be very draining. Being a target and not having any backup support can be miserably disheartening.

Later, Angela was talking to a friend that had been in that class with her. She found out that he had agreed with her stance on gun control. Since he didn't speak up, Angela had assumed he held the same hostile opinion as the rest of the class. When Angela found out he had shared her views, she was deeply hurt. She felt he had betrayed her. The truth is, he had been paralyzed with fear. He saw the way the class reacted to Angela and he simply didn't want to offer himself up as the next living sacrifice. So he kept his mouth shut and his head low. But to this day, he deeply regrets not speaking up in class.

Fear hovers over many a campus. Erin McGlinchey writes for Independent Women's Forum about being a freshman at Smith. "The Smith woman is a leader. She always says the right thing, never offends anyone and can be counted on to support the right causes. She doesn't question certain truths and she doesn't utter certain words. Forget pearls. Her necessary accessories are a pink triangle, red ribbon, black armband, and a badge promoting the cause of the moment. The Smith woman was an ideal I failed to meet as a freshman. And as I enter my senior year, I'm glad."[2]

There was a double standard at Smith, McGlinchey says. The standard of tolerance and acceptance did not apply to religious or conservative women. "The decisions these women made were constantly criticized, questioned, and mocked." McGlinchey found the double standard appalling. But she doubted anyone shared her feelings. "But I later learned that others thought as I did. In some cases, they were just too scared to speak up, but when you do speak up, it's amazing how many women will echo your sentiments."[3]

Matt Kaufman relays a similar experience from the University of Illinois. Co-founder, along with some friends, of a conservative campus newspaper called the *Illini Review*, he was denounced as bigoted, sexist, and homophobic. "Departures from the party line generally bring an automatic response," he writes. "Say that abortion kills children and you're a patriarchal oppressor of women. Say that the theory of evolution is fatally flawed and you're a religious fanatic. Say that homosexuality is immoral — or just that it's a treatable emotional disorder — and you're a homophobic hatemonger.

"None of these responses are actual arguments. They're just curses. They're not meant to describe or to analyze; they're meant to stigmatize and to silence.

"Oftentimes they work: large numbers of students either parrot the PC line or (more often) quietly avoid contradicting it. Yet political correctness looks a lot stronger on the surface than it really is. The truth is, its strength (intimidation) is also its weakness — because most people don't really *believe* in it. . . . The gods of secularism and political correctness are nothing compared to the God of Israel. They can only intimidate us if we let them — if we forget who our God is and what He does."[4]

This paralyzing fear isn't limited to college campuses. It's a national epidemic. Dr. Laura Schlessinger wrote a widely publicized column on fear titled, "America Is Afraid."

"A prime motivator for failing to stand up for what's right in your families, your schools and communities, and in your jobs, is fear. It is amazing how powerful and paralyzing fear is, especially when it's not specific.

"Like floating anxiety, it's floating fear that something bad will happen to me. Then some rational thought is brought to bear — your psychological defense mechanisms take over, and you start thinking of ways to explain your inaction, other than your own cowardice. But the bottom line is fear."[5]

Paul wrote that as Christians our attitudes are not to be a spirit of fear. "For God has not given us a spirit of timidity, but of power and love and discipline" (2 Tim. 1:7).

The more you take opportunities to speak out in class, the more you realize that intimidation is empty unless it stands on something firm. If professors wield intimidation, but can't back it up with pure and simple truth, there is no reason to fear. Fear may be the instinctive response, but it's not how God wants us to live.

First Peter 3:14–16 is quite specific about fear. "If you should suffer for the sake of righteousness, you are blessed. And do not fear their intimidation, and do not be troubled, but sanctify Christ as Lord in your hearts, always being ready to make a defense to everyone who asks you to give an account for the hope that is in you, yet with gentleness and reverence; and keep a good conscience so that in the thing in which you are slandered, those who revile your good behavior in Christ will be put to shame."

Sitting silently when truth, liberty, free speech, and tenets of Christianity are attacked is the result of fear. I understand the fear, but I also understand the need for courage. Speaking up when you'd rather not is an act of courage. Courage isn't the absence of fear, it's acting in spite of fear. Courage puts your senses on alert, your brain in gear, and a sparkle in your eye. It's the excitement that comes from living with purpose, as opposed to going with the flow.

HINDSIGHT

Go Nike.

You're sitting there thinking someone should say something, somebody should try to stop this runaway train, and yet the words stay in your mouth. When that happens, ask yourself this: If not me, then who? "C'mon. Speak up. Go Nike — Just do it.

Having Convictions.

Second Corinthians 10:15 says, "Our hope is that, as your faith continues to grow, our area of activity among you will grow greatly. . . ." Part of growing in faith involves developing your own convictions. Having convictions means being willing to be uncomfortable for the sake of an idea or a principle.

Rub a dub dub.

When faced with fear and the possibility of being embroiled in a heated discussion, remember the words of theologian G.K. Chesterton: "I believe in getting into hot water. It keeps you clean."

Fish Out of Water

From: "Liesel"

To: "Abby"

Abby,

So wonderful to her from you! I was hoping you would send a message my way.

What can I possibly say to sum up the last 5-1/2 weeks since I have left home? It was a great decision to go on the Wilderness trip that Wheaton offered 3 weeks before school started. I came back with the most amazing memories of trekking through the North Woods of Wisconsin and the Upper Peninsula of Michigan (our trip culminated on the banks of Lake Superior), established friendships with a wonderful core of friends, and two hours of class credit.

We are now in our 3rd official week of classes. My professors are really dynamic. My Political Philosophy class is amazing and I love my British Lit class. I am taking 19 hours this semester. In reality, it is only 17 because I carried in those 2 credits from the Wilderness trip.

The weather has been absolutely pristine. I have really began to find a core group of friends that I enjoy. The spiritual and intellectual depth of the student body at large has blown me away. I find myself in conversations of depth many times throughout my day. I am really enjoying the friendships that I have been able to lay foundations for. Chapel has been wonderful. Last week, we had Allistair Begg here to do special services and tonight there is going to be a debate between Gary Bauer and Tony Campolo that I am going to.

It has also been great to have the city of Chicago right here. It is a 40-minute train ride in and you can buy an all-weekend pass for nothing. I have gone into the city 3 times since being here. Over Labor Day weekend, a big group of us went in for Jazz Fest and had a great time sitting in the sun and listening to the sweet tunes of smooth jazz along the banks of Lake Michigan.

I feel that this letter isn't really satisfactory as it just gives you a sweeping generalization of my time here. I will send you more detailed accounts of the people I have met, the food fights I've had, etc. in the future.

Tell me about how things are going for you. Hope to hear from you soon.

Your friend,

Liesel

Fish Out of Water

From: "Nye, Abby"

To: "The Fam"

Hey, Fam,

I heard from Liesel. She loves Wheaton and is doing well. I keep forgetting to tell you about my friend Brooke. On the first day of English class her professor gave the class a chant he wanted them to sing. No one knew what the chant meant so Brooke asked. The professor answered: "Praise to Buddha."

Everyone in the class sang the chant except for Brooke. Brooke didn't chant because she is a Christian. Chanting praise to Buddha was disturbing to her. As the class progressed, it was also disturbing to her to see other Christians in class chanting "Praise to Buddha," then singing praise to God at Campus Crusade on Thursday nights.

After the first class when Brooke declined to participate, the professor sternly lectured the class about students who don't participate. The next class session he seemed to lighten up though and didn't make a big deal out of Brooke not chanting. The class continued to chant at the beginning of each class period throughout the semester.

I asked if the class had anything to do with religion. Brooke said "No, it was titled 'Thirteen ways to look at a blackboard.' "

Can you imagine what would have happened if the professor had passed out copies of the Doxology and asked the class to sing along?

Later gator,

Abby

I read Abby Nye Suddarth's book on college life with real interest. I believe her evaluation is quite realistic, based on what I have read from secular sources and heard from students on campuses visited since we formed ICR.

My last year at Virginia Tech (1969) was the last year of the famous "sixties" youth upheavals, and we had experienced some of those things there, though not as much as others had. Virginia Tech has always been somewhat less "liberal" (politically, that is) than other state universities.

Prior to 1970, I had been on the faculties of five secular universities, plus an invited speaker on many others, and so am somewhat familiar with campus life as it was then. Evolutionism was dominant everywhere, even more in the social sciences and humanities than in the natural-sciences. Liquor consumption was all but universal, but other drugs relatively rare. The campus religions tended to be quite liberal, but postmodernism was unheard of.

Things have surely changed in recent decades. But God had said "For they shall sow the wind, and they shall reap the whirlwind" (Hos. 8:7), and the widespread sowing of evolutionary seed in the 20th century is surely reaping bitter fruit in the 21st. We had anticipated such things would be the eventual result of the ubiquitous teaching of evolutionism in the nation's colleges and, although I can no longer speak based on firsthand knowledge, these predictions have apparently been coming to pass with a vengeance.

— Henry M. Morris, Ph.D.
President emeritus
Institute for Creation Research

Responding to Tolerance

B ig blue posters hung from the dorm and academic building walls: What the Bible REALLY says about homosexuality. It was a meeting with a gay pastor who was on campus to set the record straight. Sounded fun to me. If it's a choice between physics homework or an open discussion on homosexuality, I'll take the discussion.

The auditorium began to fill with students of all sizes, shapes, and sexual orientations. Some came with Bibles in hand, others came with someone of the same sex in hand. A large portion of the crowd was very flamboyant.

The event began as the gay pastor introduced himself. He came across as warm and friendly. He explained that he was homosexual and had been with his partner for 12 years. He then asked the audience which category each of us fit into:

Are you openly gay or lesbian? Raise your hand.

Do you think the Bible says it is wrong to live a homosexual lifestyle? Raise your hand.

Do you think the Bible says it's okay to live out a gay lifestyle? Raise your hand.

The raised hands to the last two questions were pretty evenly split. I wondered if there would be booing when those who believed the Bible does not condone a homosexual lifestyle identified themselves, but there wasn't.

The speaker opened by saying that suppressed Scriptures had been presented in an incomplete way and he was there to tell the rest of the story. And what a story it was. According to him, the real story was that Jesus healed a slave in order to sustain a gay relationship. David and Jonathan were gay and Ruth and Naomi were lesbian lovers (forget the fact that both Ruth and Naomi had been married).

His remarks were received with genuine tolerance. I'd even venture to say most of the Christians sincerely listened with open minds. But his information was false. His translations from Greek were contradictory. His basic arguments were terribly flawed. Yet, no one heckled him, jeered him, or tried to shout him down. The crowd, particularly those opposing his ideas, was truly tolerant. This was the first time I had witnessed true tolerance on the college campus. It was refreshing. This was exactly what the free exchange of ideas should look like. Christians and conservatives in the audience were tolerant of the man although they didn't agree with his ideas.

When he closed his remarks, which were 45 minutes in length, and opened the floor for questions, hands shot up in the air. As Christians and conservatives tried to get clarification on interpretations and assumptions, he grew increasingly frustrated. Audience members were making good points. They were reasoning, exposing sloppy scholarship as well as perversion of the Scriptures. He was struggling to hold his own and gradually began to lose it. Finally, in a hateful tone of voice, he said, "If you reject us by thinking homosexuality is a sin, then you'd better watch out for Judgment Day!"

His condemnation didn't make the headlines of the student newspaper or even so much as cause a stir. Can you imagine what would have happened if the tables had been turned? What if a Christian pastor had told the homosexual students they'd better watch out for Judgment Day. It would have been a classic case of hate speech.

Tolerance is a sham. Tolerance is much talked about, but rarely practiced. Tolerance, as defined by the politically correct, means tolerating those who fit snugly within the borders of the politically correct. To get a firm grasp on tolerance, and how to respond to pseudo-tolerance, we need to start with definitions.

DEFINITIONS

Webster's dictionary describes tolerance as "the act or practice of tolerating, *especially*: sympathy or indulgence for beliefs or practices differing from one's own."

The politically correct tolerance we see practiced — or rather extracted — today goes way beyond a mere sympathy or indulgence for a set of beliefs peculiar to one's own. This contemporary psuedo-tolerance has actually become a mask for intolerance.

Josh McDowell calls the phenomena of tolerance the most "ominous culture change in human history." He says, "It is a change so vast that its implications are mind-boggling. Most frightening of all is that most Christians seem to be missing it. As a result, we may very well wake up in the not-too-distant future in a culture that is not only unreceptive but openly hostile to the Church and the gospel of Jesus Christ, a culture in which those who proclaim the gospel will be labeled as bigots and fanatics, a culture in which persecution of Christians will be not only allowed but applauded. And all of it will be directly related to the 'new tolerance.' "[1]

Christians themselves are very confused. One study McDowell cites reveals that "the majority of kids (57%) in strong, evangelical churches already believe what the new tolerance is teaching: that what is wrong for one person is not necessarily wrong for someone else."[2] Score one for moral relativism.

Does the Bible talk about tolerance? In the NIV, the word "forbearance" is sometimes translated tolerance. In the original Greek, the word for tolerance means to hold up, as in "forbearing with one another." The concept of tolerance is biblical. We are commanded to forbear with one another, and to be patient with one another in the interest of growth, maturity, and coming to discover truth. Tolerance and forbearance in pursuit of a worthwhile goal are good things. Yet, with all the commotion this new form of tolerance causes, the very word almost leaves a bad taste in one's mouth.

I was trying to think of examples of how the politically correct are tolerant on a secular college campus, but most of the examples involve being tolerant of deviancy and immorality. My fitness instructor promoted tolerance and diversity by encouraging us to go watch a drag show. She was telling us which bars to catch the shows at when she realized that as freshmen we were all under 21. Being a responsible faculty member, she said we should wait until we were 21 and *then* go see a drag show. She said she would encourage us to see drag shows just like she would encourage us to visit a place of different ethnicity.

The politically correct often exercise their version of tolerance by accusing those with opposing views of intolerance. Had I suggested viewing a drag show might not contribute to one's lifetime fitness, I surely would have been accused of being intolerant.

It is important to understand this because identifying and labeling intolerance in others is the nucleus of the tolerance movement. By pointing out those who are intolerant, the tolerant create an illusion of moral superiority. They market themselves as self-righteous, the holy ones, the people that "truly" care, that "truly" understand and have a corner on the market of truth — if there was such a thing as truth. Of course, the guardians of tolerance, by being intolerant of others, are actually practicing the thing they preach against — but let's not confuse them with reality.

Much of the nonsense in the classroom, the lunacy of freshman orientation, and the garbage at large that happens on a college campus today is made possible by this great myth of tolerance. That's why it is important to understand how tolerance works, and to follow the faulty premises of tolerance to their disastrous logical ends.

THE TWO LIES

The myth of tolerance is fueled by two major lies. You may not recognize these lies when you first encounter them. Initially, they may even sound good and make sense. But when you subject them to the scrutiny of basic reasoning, the lies become apparent.

The first lie is that tolerant people are good people and that intolerant people are bad people. Inherent in this idea is that tolerance is always good. Therefore, the more tolerant a person is, the better a human being that person becomes.

Really? Why don't we try it out.

Let's say you are a male at college and your roommate wants his girlfriend to spend the night in your dorm room. You tolerate that with a wink and a nod, and hey, you're cool. You're tolerant. Who are you to judge?

Let's say the next night, he wants to have two girls spend the night. You might be a little more uncomfortable with this scenario, and it's not really your thing, but that doesn't mean it can't be your roommate's thing. And besides, you've already proven yourself tolerant of one girl and earned the accolade of good guy. By extending the logic of tolerance, if you tolerate two girls, you become twice as tolerant and twice as good. You are doubly understanding. Doubly less judgmental and doubly compassionate.

Now, let's say the roommate is tired of sexual escapades in the dorm room with two girls at a time and wants to try something different. Really different. Maybe bring a sheep in the room. Or a cow. Or a little boy. You now have an incredible opportunity to prove just how open-minded and truly tolerant you really are. You can see how once started down the path of tolerance, you begin veering down a slippery slope. Tolerance is not the equivalent of goodness. Blind tolerance without discretion is anything but good. It's ignorant. G.K. Chesterton referred to tolerance as the virtue that remains after a man has lost all his principle.

The truth is, most of the people who give lip service to tolerance don't believe in it themselves. They can't quite put their finger on it, but they know in their gut there's something bogus. In some cases they simply haven't thought it through. In other cases, they have thought it through, but they're too scared to talk. Too afraid of being labeled intolerant.

SECOND LIE

The second lie about tolerance wraps itself around the first. The second lie goes like this: Just because it's wrong for me, doesn't mean it's wrong for you. No thoughts, ideas, or value judgments are better than any others. No set of ideas, convictions, or principles have more merit than another. This, again, is the heart of moral relativism. There is no right or wrong, no absolute truth, morality changes relative to the winds of culture. One day it may be illegal to kill babies in the womb, one day it may not. One day it may be illegal to snuff out grandma in the nursing home, one day it may not.

On occasion, my initial reaction to this assumption that all ideas have equal worth has been to think, *Who am I to say my Christian convictions are good and noble?* On second thought, there are approximately 2,000 years of tradition behind my Christian principles. They embody the principles of natural law. They have been the foundation for the institutions of marriage and family that have sustained cultures, and for 2,500 years the Judeo-Christian tradition that has created one of the longest-lasting moral orders in the history of man.

The concept that all convictions, principles, and ideas have equal merit, and nobody's idea is better than somebody else's idea, carries a mighty intimidation factor. But if you take the reasoning and apply it to other situations, the fallacy becomes apparent.

Was there no difference between Sadam Hussein's conviction that dissidents should be jailed, tortured, and have their eyes gouged out, and our founding fathers' conviction that dissidents have the right to free speech? Was there no difference between Hitler's conviction that the Jews are an inferior race and need to be exterminated, and the United State's conviction that ethnic cleansing is immoral? Both ideas cannot be equal in merit. Both ideas do not yield equal consequences.

Fundamental to the success of the lie that all ideas have equal worth is viewing life apart from a framework that includes God. When there is no moral authority in your view of life, it's easy to see how this lie takes hold. If man is the one writing truth, not God, and all men are created equal (so says the Declaration of Independence) then all truths must be equal.

Following such logic, the truth claims of the Klu Klux Klan are just as valid as the truth claims of Dr. Martin Luther King. The philosophy of Stalin is just as valid as the philosophy of Plato. The belief systems of Hitler, Lenin, and Saddam Hussein are just as valid as those of C.S. Lewis, Churchill, and Mother Teresa. Ludicrous. Following such logic doesn't just lead to chaos on a college campus, it leads to chaos in the world at large.

The mush mind of tolerance leads to "group think." Individuals become too intimidated to think for themselves and eventually *unable* to think for themselves. Fear takes over and the risk of speaking up seems too great. That fear leads to an abridgement of freedom of speech, the very cornerstone of liberty. Without exaggeration, I believe that on many college campuses, in many classrooms, in many settings, the fear of speaking and going against the grain border on the fear more commonly found in a dictatorship or police state.

As Christians, we can't be passive spectators when it comes to tolerance. When a Christian says, "This is what I believe to be true, but you can believe what you want to be true," Christianity is demeaned. Certainly that person has a right to believe what he or she wants, but you don't have to do that "agree to disagree" business.

Fish Out of Water

Two opposing truths cannot be simultaneously true. Christianity claims to be the Truth, capital T. Narrow? Oh, yeah. Gonna raise eyebrows? Definitely.

Christianity is a logical target for tolerance watchdogs because, in one sense, Christianity is intolerant. Jesus claimed to be the Way, the Truth, and the Life. He claimed to be the only Son of God. Those aren't exactly claims that are vague or ambiguous. He didn't describe himself as one of many ways to God, but *the* way. This is just the kind of statement that makes tolerance watchdogs foam at the mouth and strain at the leash. So on the one hand, we can say with certainty that Christianity is intolerant. Well, we can say it, but it's not entirely true.

There is also a dynamic of Christianity that is very tolerant. Christianity may be one of the most tolerant religions in the world.

How so? Christianity is tolerant in that Christ accepts men and women in whatever moral and spiritual state they are in. You don't have to get your act together, pass a test, or prove yourself before you can come to Christ. If you have a problem with drugs, you're welcome to come. Problem with alcohol? You're welcome, too. If you have a problem with honesty, cheating, a horrible temper, or an eating disorder, or you're in a relationship that's a mess, you're welcome.

The core of the gospel message is that Jesus died for all men. There are no stipulations extending grace and redemption to a certain few of a particular race, gender, class, or social status. No one is excluded. The invitation is truly tolerant, because the invitation is for all.

The beauty of this invitation is that you can come in a terrible state, but God won't leave you in a terrible state. He'll give you a rock to cling to, firm ground to stand on, and heal you from the inside out. That is true tolerance in the classic sense of the word — a forbearing that works toward growth and maturity.

FAILURE TO DEAL WITH TOLERANCE

When we fail to deal with the tolerance issue, two things happen. As conservatives, we compromise liberty. As Christians, we compromise truth. Those are the two things at risk when we silently bow to leftist tolerance.

So, how do college students deal with the problem of psuedo-tolerance? Based on my own experiences, including some mistakes, I offer the following ideas.

1. Start with courage.

Get off the sidelines, jump in, and play ball. Muster the courage and determine to speak up. Not all the time, not every time. Engage as a player instead of a spectator. Resolve that you will speak up. Secondly, resolve that when another Christian speaks up, especially if it's not going well for him or her, that you will speak up and support that person. "And if one can overpower him who is alone, two can resist him" (Eccles. 4:12).

2. Stay cool.

Once you've determined to speak, how you speak is just as important. It can't be arrogantly or self-righteously, but it can be with enthusiasm and great passion. The key is not to get so caught up in the debate that you get angry. If you start to feel the anger build (your heart races, you feel flushed, and you'd really, really like to "reach out and touch someone"), let it go. Stay calm. The minute you succumb to anger, the discussion is over and you lose. Composure is everything. The goal is not to win debates and leave your opponent in shreds. The goal is to get other people to think, to consider your point of view, and to reconsider their own.

3. Focus on principles, not people.

The Bible says to be prepared with a ready answer. It's hard to prepare answers when you don't know what the questions are going to be. What's also amazing is how fast the questions come when these discussions unfold. It's rapid fire. In those situations, the best thing to do is try to separate out a single principle, think of it as a thread if you will, and follow it. Once you've separated out the one thread you want to focus on, be sure to maintain a separation between the principle and the people. Don't let others force you to generalize. Don't let the other side frame the argument. Make clear distinctions between people and principles. This is critical. You don't want to condemn people, you want to discuss principles. Isolate the principle and follow it to its logical end. Point out that ideas have consequences.

4. Dismantle the "judging charge" as soon as it arises.

Often in these lively discussions, the first charge lobbed is that you are judging and the Bible says do not judge. Taken out of context, "judge not" sounds like a universal statement against ever making a judgment. The greater context is hypocrisy and pride. We should not judge with the goal of putting ourselves on a higher spiritual plane and we should not judge by a standard we are unwilling to apply to ourselves.

Judging, in an eternal sense, is the business of God. The passage does not preclude people from ever making a judgment, because right after the verses that warn about judging is this one: "Do not give what is holy to dogs, and do not throw your pearls before swine." You'd have to make some judgments to determine what is holy, who the dogs are, and who the pigs are.

Further, if "judge not" is a universal ban, positive judgments would be taboo as well as negative judgments. We couldn't judge that a movie was good, a book excellent, or a lecture challenging. As Elisabeth Elliott writes on this matter, "If we were not to judge at all we would have to expunge from our Christian vocabulary the word *is*, for whatever follows that word is a judgment. Jack is a fine yachtsman, Mrs. Smith is a cook, Harold is a bum. . . . Jesus told us to love our enemies. How are we to know who they are without judgment? He spoke of dogs, swine, hypocrites, liars, as well as of friends, followers, rich men, the great and the small, the humble and the proud, 'he who hears you and he who rejects you,' old and new wineskins, the things of the world and the things of the Kingdom. To make any sense at all of these teachings requires, among other things, the God-given faculty of judgment, which includes discrimination."[3]

Make it clear that we are all judgmental. Each one of us makes judgments each and every day, both positive judgments and negative judgments.

5. Limit the Bible thumping.

One Saturday morning I attended part of an ordination service for two new pastors at our church. A council of pastors and elders asked them questions about doctrine and theology to test their worthiness for ordination. It was a wonderful process of Q and A as the candidates for ordination responded to questions about the problem of evil, the make-up of the trinity, and many other theological issues. Naturally, they built their answers based on Scripture. It struck me that that kind of dialogue doesn't work in the college classroom.

The key is to find a common denominator. When Paul spoke to the pagans on Mars Hill, he didn't quote Old Testament Scripture. Paul was an Old Testament scholar, but that's not the reference point he used on Mars Hill. He considered the audience, pagans fond of the poets, and he himself quoted the pagan poets. He found the reference point of his peers and worked from there.

Apollos was "mighty in the scriptures" (Acts 18:24) and powerfully refuted the Jews in public, demonstrating by the Scriptures that Jesus was the Christ. Apollos knew his audience and knew what they respected — the Scriptures — so that became his common denominator. Two very different audiences; two very different approaches. Know your audience and speak their language.

What's the common denominator for most people? Basic right and wrong. People may deny that they believe in the absolutes that determine right and wrong, but, deep down, almost everybody does

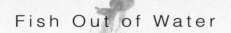

believe in absolutes that determine right and wrong. Every culture in the world intrinsically knows it's wrong to murder. It is important to appeal to that sense of right and wrong deep within individuals. Romans says that God has written the basics of right and wrong on every man's heart (Rom. 1:19–20). Appeal to a base of right and wrong and work from there.

6. Be encouraging.

Try to end the discourse on a positive note. You don't have to ingratiate yourself to anybody, or compromise your principles, but try to end on a civil tone (even if they don't — *especially* if they don't). The goal is not to obliterate people in a war of words — the goal is to win a few more people over to your way of thinking. Annihilation usually isn't the best method for doing that.

7. Smile.

Why? Because you're right.

HINDSIGHT

Keep the two lies in mind.

The first lie is that tolerant people are good people and that intolerant people are bad people. The second lie says: Just because it's wrong for you, doesn't mean it's wrong for me. No thoughts, ideas, or value judgments are better than any others.

Be swift.

Calmly respond to the charge of intolerance or "being judgmental" immediately. Don't allow others to distort the truth and stick a label on you.

Use logic.

Take absurd premises — "what may be right for you, may not be right for me" — to absurd conclusions.

Be authentic.

Be passionate. Be authentic. But be respectful and kind. Sometimes it's not what you say, but how you say it. Name-calling and anger mean you're out of ideas and out of patience. When you are sincere, you may be thought of as someone who is approachable, and this may open the door to further discussions.

Fish Out of Water

From: "Sarah"

To: "Abby"

Hi Abby,

I am a senior at Ohio State University. Attending this university has been one of the biggest challenges to my faith. I know God called me to be a light in a very dark place here at OSU. Whether its reaching out to a classmate and simply listening to their problems and praying for them, or tackling the "difficult" issues like evolution and homosexuality inside the classroom, God has called Christian students to stand up for His truth and message of forgiveness and love. Unfortunately, I have seen too many of my own Christian classmates shrink back from voicing opinions in biology or sociology and psychology classes simply because they are afraid of being labeled a "Jesus Freak Conservative." It is a tough atmosphere to be placed in, but that is no excuse for us to shrink back and let false teachings be spread without a fight.

God doesn't give us more than we can handle, and if He has called students to a secular university then He is simply waiting for them to ask and rely on His strength and wisdom on how to approach issues.

His,

Sarah

From: "Kari"

To: "Abby"

Abby,

Maybe being a Christian and a conservative is hard on a secular campus, but on a Christian campus you run into just as many moral issues. You soon learn about the people with the connections and the stories from last year about those who didn't come back for whatever reasons. Soon you hear of resident assistants being removed from their positions for either letting too many things get by or because they themselves initiated such events. I was appalled since I see the RAs as spiritual leaders and how they took the responsibility lightly. I was invited to a party that was off campus at someone's brother's house. I already knew about other parties that had taken place there that weren't good. I came up with a reason for not attending and two days later found out the whole story. There was a lot of alcohol and the short of it is that all the people who went to the party have been called to a meeting to discuss consequences for their actions. You can never assume that a Christian college is immune to such happenings. But I would hope the incidents are less likely to occur here than at a secular college. When I say no to an invitation, suddenly I am uptight and legalistic and I just don't know how to have fun. I don't care what they call me, I will still say no.

Well anyway, class calls.

Kari

Christians in secular colleges and universities can expect to encounter opposition if they major in a field of science. Secular professors will often present arguments designed to undermine the Bible. These might include arguments which supposedly support evolution, the big bang, a multi-billion-year-old earth, and attempt to undermine the biblical teachings of creation in six days and the global Flood. It is very important that we are able to refute these criticisms — not only for our own conviction, but for the sake of others. We need to be ready to give an answer and defend our faith (1 Pet. 3:15).

When I was in college and graduate school, the resources and web articles at Answers in Genesis (AnswersinGenesis.org) and ICR really helped me to be informed on the issues so that I could see the problems in the evolutionists' arguments. By being informed on the issues, I understood that when the evidence is interpreted correctly, it always supports a straightforward reading of the Bible. I learned about many Ph.D. scientists who reject the big bang and instead believe that God created, just as the Bible teaches. Although Christians will face open hostility from some of their secular peers and many of their evolutionist professors, there is no need to be afraid of the evidence itself. The scientific evidence confirms the Bible.

— Jason Lisle, Ph.D.

Pick Your Battles

O f all things that surprised and shocked me at college, the one-sidedness of so many classroom discussions was the most surprising of all. The lack of balance, the lack of honest exploration, the lack of real, unbiased and open discussion was not how I thought it would be. It was like that bold dynamic of education had silently melded with the white wallboard or slid out the crack between the window and the sill and evaporated among the clouds in the bright blue sky.

When I thought about why I expected such analysis and discussion, aside from the fact that it had once been a staple of a basic college education, I realized it was due to the high school I had attended.

I graduated from a private Christian high school. My high school, while founded and guided by the "narrow" principles of Christianity, was truly more diverse in thought than this secular college campus could ever pretend to be. More than two hundred different churches were represented at my high school. That's a slew of denominations, break-off denominations, and splinter denominations, and a host of views on important and sometimes controversial doctrinal issues.

In an attempt to accommodate that paradox of diversity and unity, the guiding principle was always truth. The means for finding truth was honest scholarship. Our Bible instructors, the ones most often called to keep a keen eye on that delicate balance between diversity and unity, would present historical views on a matter that had potential to be divisive or controversial. They would also present contemporary views, opposing views, and sometimes even invite speakers from opposite camps in to be interviewed by the class. Then, they would do something revolutionary. They would let us think.

Our instructors encouraged us to consider all the views, reason our way through them, and draw our own conclusions. Unlike some of my college classes, where the professors eagerly, enthusiastically, and forcefully shared *their* viewpoint and neglected to mention other viewpoints, my high school teachers often opted not to share their personal opinions. When asked, sometimes they would tell what their position was on an issue, but never with the intent of forcing the class to adopt the same view. We were always welcome to stay after class if we wanted to know what they specifically believed about a particular issue.

I expected intellectual honesty and intellectual freedom from the faculty when I went to college. But a lot of times there was no routine standard of honest exploration of controversial issues, it was often a pat answer PC. As rigorous or deep as many discussions got was "agreeing to disagree," a most nauseating principle in that the unspoken thought behind it was often that truth is unattainable. So many things were left of center, no questions asked. There was one side to every story and nobody seemed interested in hearing the other side(s). Many professors are not as interested in teaching students *how* to think as they are in teaching students *what* to think.

Part of the problem is that there are no checks and balances. If a liberal professor wants to indoctrinate, he or she can freely do so, without restraint, behind the secrecy of closed doors, climbing ivy, and brick walls. David Horowitz, a nationally known academic and civil liberties activist comments, "Universities are among our most important social institutions. They educate our youth, train future leaders, provide information and research, advance scientific and medical knowledge, generate technological innovation, and shape the attitudes that define us as a people. Yet universities are also anomalies in our national framework. Vital as they are to the functioning of our democracy, they are themselves undemocratic.

"Overall, there is little or no accountability on the part of these institutions to the wider community that supports them and underwrite the affluence to which their principals have become accustomed. Whether private or public, whether operating under the aegis of state-appointed boards or private corporations, universities are effectively ruled by internal bureaucracies, which operate under a cloak of secrecy and are protected from oversight by privileges and traditions that date back to feudal times.

"What is knowledge if it is thoroughly one-sided, or intellectual freedom if it is only freedom to conform? And what is a liberal education, if one point of view is for all intents and purposes excluded from the classroom?"

Then, Horowitz poses an excellent question I have often asked myself: "How can students get a good education, if they are only being told one side of the story?"[1]

At some point, students (and their parents) must ask, what's the point of a broad-based liberal education, if you're exposed to a narrow perspective? As Horowitz has stated, "If you only get half the picture, you only get half the education." And as many others, like Horowitz, have asked, "Does it not therefore follow that students should only pay half the tuition?" Somehow I don't think that idea is going to go over too well.

Fish Out of Water

University of Kansas professor Dennis Dailey has tried to push the limits in his human sexuality class. Students have reported that he used porn movies, graphic slides of naked children, crude language in class, and directed sexually insulting remarks to his students. He even had a Pedophilia Day and a Wheelchair Sex Day. Last year, Dailey was honored as an outstanding educator by the university. This was going on at a school funded by parents and taxpayers. No doubt many parents — and taxpayers — have some objections about the way their money is being spent.

As I've taken my core classes, required of all students for graduation, it has been my experience that there is a far heavier concentration of liberals in the social sciences than in the hard sciences. My professors in chemistry, biology, and physics generally stick to the subject matter and rarely digress into political and social ideologue irrelevant to the class. There is, however, considerable personal opinion injected into classes like psychology.

Take the class where we spent 20 minutes viewing slides of primates. The professor would flash a slide on the screen and ask, "Does this monkey look sad, happy, about to attack?" Picture after picture of the faces of primates were flashed on the screen. "How about this monkey? Is he happy, sad, angry?" The point of this was to prove that we come from primates because we have the same facial expressions. On and on, chimp after chimp. After each slide he would tell us exactly what the ape was thinking and feeling. After 20 minutes of sad, happy, angry, jealous, and contented chimps, monkeys, and apes, he led us to the conclusion that, because apes emote, and we emote, we therefore came from apes.

Oh, well, at least the slide show was a break from lecture. And at least sitting in the dark meant we didn't have to see what T-shirt the professor had pulled from his drawer that day. Previously, he had come to class with a T-shirt that said, "World's Fastest Swimmer." On the back of the T-shirt was a picture of a sperm.

I had a T-shirt I sometimes thought about wearing to class, but I never did. My T-shirt said, "Never Underestimate the Power of

Stupid People in Large Groups." No picture on the back. You have to keep a sense of humor about these things or you end up taking yourself too seriously.

DARE TO DEBATE

When you inject an opinion into a class discussion that is at odds with the professor's, know that there are a variety of techniques professors use to rebuff dissenters and steer the discussion back in their direction. Sometimes the technique may be hostility, mocking, or sarcasm. Other times the technique is more gentle. It is a subtle redirect, but it is a redirect nonetheless. One particular professor used laughter and a big smile to curtail the discussion.

More than once in my class on Islam, I would bring up a different point of view and the professor would laugh and say, "Oh, we won't talk about that."

One day we learned that Muslims believe that God is in every person. The professor thought this was a really nice idea and obviously embraced the idea.

It *is* a nice idea, but I asked if it didn't present a problem. "If Muslims believe Christians go to hell, and if God is in everyone — including Christians — then aren't they banishing God to hell?"

Once again, she laughed and said she really couldn't answer that. (She's a Harvard grad.) I think she could have answered the question. She could have answered it coming from either side, but for fear of undermining the Islamic faith or offending Muslims, although there were none in the class, she steered clear of the issue.

Another day we were discussing the separation of church and state. No one was saying much; there seemed to be a silent consensus that separation of church and state was a good and necessary thing. An education major then spoke up and raised the issue of vouchers. The professor said, "Do you really want government money paying for someone to get a religious education?"

I said that I believed public schools were just as religious as some private schools. People looked over at me and asked, "How?"

I said, "Because secular humanism was declared an official religion in 1961." The prof began talking over me as soon as I uttered the word humanism. She said once we bring humanism into the discussion it would destroy her argument. "We won't bring that into the picture," she said. End of discussion. She was nice and friendly and polite, but the discussion was over. It's a shame she didn't pursue the matter, because she seemed like a professor with the academic integrity to present all sides and lead a civilized discussion.

During another class lecture, the same prof was trying to say that the Christian God and the Islamic God were the same. A group of Christians in class disagreed and tried to make the point that Christians believe in the deity of Jesus Christ, therefore, it can't be the same God if part of the godhead is missing. She said, "It's really not all that different. Yes, Muslims don't believe Jesus Christ was God, but Jesus Christ didn't believe He was God."

A student said, "Some of us are pretty sure Jesus did think He was God."

The prof said, "It's not in the Bible. Prove it."

"In the beginning was the Word, and the Word was with God, and the Word was God," someone said. "He who has seen Me, has seen the Father," I said.

The professor shot the references down and said we had a poor understanding of Scripture. She didn't laugh, she just flatly rejected the evidence.

Over the next couple of days, I looked up references on the deity of Christ in Josh McDowell's book, *Answers to Tough Questions Skeptics Ask about the Christian Faith*. I typed up two pages of notes, largely from the McDowell book, regarding verses and arguments about Jesus being God and knowing He is God.

I gave the professor a copy of my notes the next week in class. I also gave copies to four friends in other sections of the same class, as I knew they were having similar discussions with different professors. It helps to network with other Christians and share resources and information.

For a number of days after I gave that information to my prof, she would come up to me at the beginning of class and say, "I'm still thinking about that." She also thanked me for putting in extra work on that issue and has repeatedly said that it was very interesting.

Even though a professor may not always give you an opportunity to be heard in class, he or she may still have an open mind. There may be other opportunities outside of class for you to express your opinion. If a professor knows that you are sincere about an issue, if you show that you care about the issue, and if you demonstrate that you are serious in your pursuit of the truth, in some cases a professor will take you seriously.

FRUSTRATION

In a philosophy class, the professor often engaged in Bushwhacking, taking swipes at President Bush and the "right-wing born-again Christian staff" that "runs his show" as though the president and Christians were inextricably linked. I attempt to project a pretty calm and reserved appearance in class and manifest a loving spirit, but some days when this tripe went on, and let me add that I *really* liked this professor, I would fantasize about knocking over my desk and walking out of the classroom without saying a word. Just for grins. Could be fun.

One day, upset at the looming war with Iraq, and apparently frustrated that the Resolution for Peace she had attached her name to in the student newspaper, along with a number of other faculty members, wasn't going to stop the tanks from rolling, she again began Bush-whacking. After a brief rant, she became sidetracked on a tangent. She started talking, to herself more than to the class, in a soft voice about creationists. "Most Christians don't believe in creationism and most large churches don't teach creationism," she said. She continued on, saying, "People who actually believe in creationism are quaint . . . they're like Amish."

(Bam! A second desk goes flying.)

Some of the philosophy professor's asides were so entertaining I wish I had a tape player in class with me to capture every word. But at the bottom of our syllabus it said, "Unless you are a disabled student, tape recorders are not permitted in this class." Ah, but I am a disabled student (in their eyes). I am a student who believes in God, the saving work of Christ, and moral absolutes.

PICKING YOUR BATTLES

Every class will not be a battle, but it's important to be prepared for when a challenge does arise. Knowing how to be selective about your battles, how to engage, which ones to engage in, and which ones to pass on, will be valuable. You don't have to voice your opinion on every single issue. In some classes, there simply wouldn't be enough time! And in some cases, the right thing to do is keep your mouth closed. But when the time is right and you feel the nudge to voice your opinion or debate in the classroom, there are certain things that are beneficial to know.

KNOW YOU WON'T WIN THE ARGUMENT

That's right, chances are you're not going to win the argument. At least, not in the classroom. Most likely you won't convince the professor to change his views. Professors are usually set in stone about their beliefs and if you do impact their thinking, they're not about to admit it to the class. The fact that you will most likely not win an argument though is not reason enough to remain quiet.

Winning and losing take on new meanings when engaging with different world views in the classroom. Winning doesn't just have to be about changing the professor's beliefs. Winning could be the simple, but difficult task of getting professors to question their beliefs. What's more, losing an argument does not come without benefits. By speaking up in class you are registering dissent. You are making the professor aware that not everyone thinks the way he or she does. By speaking up, you may also plant seeds of doubt in the professor's mind, and just as important, in the minds of your fellow classmates. Your speaking up can mean opening up the door to explore other options and giving people both sides of an issue so that they can come to their own educated opinion. By speaking up, you also may win over some fence sitters without ever being aware of your impact. Finally, by speaking up, you will be encouraging those who are quiet so that they may gain the courage to do the same.

KNOW THE FIELDS WITH WHICH YOU ARE MOST COMFORTABLE

The reason students go to college is to learn. It would be unrealistic to think that students are well versed on every topic — especially one about which you have chosen to take a class. It's normal to feel hesitant to speak up because of lack of knowledge on an issue. But once again, that is not a sufficient excuse to back down when absolute truth is being attacked. The worst that could happen is someone will ask you a question that you don't know the answer to. All you have to do is say, "I really don't know the answer to that." Your honesty will speak for itself. You could even go a little further and put the ball back in the other person's court by saying "If you're really looking for that answer, there's a good book out that addresses this issue." Most often, the professor is trapped into admitting he doesn't care what the answer is because his mind is made up already. Or, there's always the chance, a slim one but still a chance, that the prof may express interest in reading a book you suggest, which opens the door to continuing dialog throughout the semester.

When speaking up in class, it is generally helpful to know which fields you are most comfortable talking about. Is it a Christian world view as it relates to sanctity of life, same sex marriage, prophecy proofs, the life of Christ, apologetics, faith and the founding fathers, bioethics, or faith in the marketplace? You will be bringing your own unique background and experiences to the classroom that others can benefit from. Perhaps you have volunteered at a Crisis Pregnancy Center and abortion is an issue that you are comfortable talking about. Find the subjects, issues, and current events you are passionate about and educate yourself. You will be more comfortable speaking up in class when you are speaking with both your mind and your heart.

What are the issues that fuel your passion? They vary from person to person, but typically they will be the issues that, when wrongly presented in class, tug at your heart or crawl under your skin. Nobody can be an expert on all things, so develop a topic or two you are comfortable discussing.

KNOW THE BEST APPROACH

You have teeth, right? Show them. Not in a growl, in a smile. I have found that posing dissent with a question and a smile is the best approach. For example, if the discussion topic in class is same-sex marriage, and as a Christian you know the act of homosexuality is a sin, you can speak up by saying "Well, if two guys are allowed to get married, then what prevents three guys from getting married? Or a man and a boy? Or a man and an animal?" Smile while you're asking the question. Professors respond more favorably when dissent is in the form of a friendly question instead of an angry student simply yelling, "Same sex marriages are wrong!" This question and smile approach works because you show that you are interested in the topic, interested in the ramifications of the professor's beliefs, and are honestly interested in deeper discussion. Asking questions also works in your favor because it puts the burden of proof on the one being questioned. The professor is now faced with the challenge of backing up what he or she believes.

KNOW WHEN TO KEEP QUIET

Sometimes Christians get bad reps because they don't know when enough is enough. Some Christians find it hard to know when to start; others find it hard to know when to stop. Be aware of that. There is no use in beating a dead horse. Once you have voiced your opinion on an issue, you don't need to (and probably shouldn't) keep interrupting class every time the issue comes up. If you speak up once, you've already gone on record and people know what you think. It's no longer necessary to shoot your hand in the air and say the same thing every time the issue is at hand. Speak up when it's important. Trust your instincts and the nudging of the Holy Spirit.

After Islam class one day, my professor called me aside and gave me a magazine page she had clipped out. She said she ran across something I might be interested in reading. She handed me a clip from *Newsweek* with a quote circled on the page that read, " 'I actually think Bush is the greatest threat to life on this planet,' London Mayor Ken Livingston, saying he refuses to recognize George W. Bush as the lawful president of the United States." I chuckled, smiled, and walked out of class. What I found ironic was that I had never expressed political opinions in that class. Because of the religious nature of the course, she knew I was a Christian, and a conservative at that. She knew where I stood, so I didn't need to keep hammering the same old points, I needed to stay silent and gain her respect by doing well in the class.

DON'T TAKE IT PERSONALLY

Treat everyone with respect. If you find yourself in a hostile environment with name-calling, rise above it and don't retaliate. When you show respect to others and that respect is not returned, don't take it personally. When others disagree with you, don't take it personally. (By the way, this is much, much easier to say than to do.) When you're called intolerant and closed-minded, don't take it personally. (See previous parenthetical comment.) Depending on your personality, this may be a challenge or this may be no big deal. It took me a while to get used to the feeling. At first I was very upset and discouraged when people vehemently disagreed with me, called me names, or started flinging labels, but it helped to realize that it was really the truth that they were objecting to, not me.

TRUTH IN LOVE

Every college campus is full of people longing to be loved. Take every opportunity in the classroom, and out of the classroom to show professors and fellow classmates love. This doesn't mean backing down on truth. Sometimes it means loving them enough to speak the truth. It also helps to go out of your way to do acts of kindness. In *The New Tolerance,* Josh McDowell writes, "I am convinced as Christian students strive to show extra-mile kindness to professors who are antagonistic to the faith, the charm of the new tolerance will seem shallow compared to the power of true Christian love." There aren't a lot of opportunities to go the extra mile in an hour lecture class, but don't pass them by when they do arise. Occasionally, professors ask for volunteers to carry papers or projects back to the office, or they ask for a volunteer to collect the evaluations and place them in the appropriate place at the end of each semester. It's not a big deal, but in the rush of college life a professor notices a student who gives up five minutes to help.

KNOWING YOUR STYLE

Personalities play a role in your approach to debate and discussion. Your style of interaction in the classroom may be different from your style of interaction with your peers. Different situations, different voices, different approaches.

Knowing Your Style — In the Classroom

Obviously, a shy person may not feel as comfortable speaking up as an outgoing person does. While there are a variety ways to express your opinion and stay clear of the limelight in class, at one point or another all Christian students at secular universities will be faced with speaking up, regardless of their personality characteristics. As one who has spoken up and stood alone, I would encourage all Christian students to speak up. You don't have to say something profound or long, just say you disagree with the non-Christian or immoral view being offered as truth. Other times you will need to speak up to support another student leading the charge. You may have butterflies in your stomach, a knot in your throat, and sweaty palms, but afterward you won't regret taking a stand for Christ. The following are ways you can take a stand whether you are outgoing and gregarious or timid and shy.

Use Your Voice

For the student that is outgoing, the easiest approach will be to speak up in class. Follow the guidelines above and remember to show utmost respect to the professor, no matter how little respect you have for his opinion.

Support Outspoken Christians

If you're not as comfortable speaking up in class, hopefully someone else will initiate dialog so you don't have to. If a Christian in your class voices his opinion, you can assume a different role. Make the effort to find that person and tell them you appreciate what they had to say and that you were thinking the same thing. The person who spoke up was probably apprehensive to begin with and will be very encouraged by a little affirmation and support.

Approach the Professor after Class

Not all situations are conducive to interrupting lectures, so it's best to hold certain comments until after class. Students who aren't typically outgoing may find it easier to approach the professor one-on-one after class, rather than drawing the attention of the whole class. Professors tend to be a little more relaxed and approachable after class anyway.

Debrief with Friends

If it's still impossible to muster up the guts to speak up in, or after, class try to debrief with friends from that class. Start conversations about what the professor said. Find out what other people think. Analyze how the prof's views promote moral relativism. You're sure to run into other people who think critically and, once you do, you can support each other when you're weary of a professor who constantly harps on Christianity.

Knowing Your Style — In Relationships on Campus

In addition to knowing the correct approach in the classroom, you will be faced with new challenges of how to approach and relate to friends and acquaintances on campus that are non-Christians. One of the most important qualities a student can possess in order to survive and thrive on a secular campus is to be what Bill Hybels and Mark Mittelberg call a "contagious Christian." If you live the full life of a committed Christian, becoming a contagious Christian will come naturally. Your actions will speak for themselves. Sometimes an additional step must be taken to tell people why you are different, why you do certain things, and don't do other things. In Hybels and Mittelberg's must-read book, *Becoming a Contagious Christian,* Hybels says, "I've learned through the years that seekers are not impressed with spinelessness. I need to emphasize this because many Christians are so afraid that if they state what they really believe, if they come out of the closet, or if they live by biblical priorities, then they'll automatically alienate those outside the faith. But that's almost never the case." He goes on to explain, "When a believer speaks up for what is right, defends Christianity intelligently, or lives his faith openly and authentically, seekers are forced to deal with the implications for their own lives."

It would be misleading for me to give the impression that the only job of a Christian student on a secular campus is evangelism. It will be a significant part of campus life as a Christian, but so will your studies, involvement in extracurricular activities, and a host of other things that can keep a college student too busy to do laundry for two weeks. Because of the time crunch common to college students, sharing your faith often will mean a sacrifice of your time. It may mean staying up later to finish studying or skipping a meal to continue a conversation with a seeking friend. My experience has been that God seems to ambush my scheduled time in order to remind me that my days are His. So are yours. Countless times, spiritual conversations arise, friends need a listening ear, or distressed friends call on the phone during what was supposed to be serious study time. I have to ask myself what is more important, studying or building relationships. You also have to factor in that God puts people in unique circumstances to be used by Him and we should keep our eyes open for those opportunities. The chance to guide a non-Christian friend may not come again, but the chance to study usually will.

Reaching and impacting non-Christians has to be preceded by what I call the "Starbucks First" principle. We have a Starbucks on campus and it is very easy to meet people there and spend an hour or two in conversation. Invest time in getting to know your friends on a personal level without bringing up religion. Don't jump the gun by trying to "save their souls" without getting to know them and be a friend first.

Investing time in your friends' lives often forges these connections. If your friend is involved in the glee club, gospel choir, or theater, go see their concerts or productions. If a friend has a need, find a way to help meet it. The most common way this comes up at college is with cars. If you have wheels, you're going to have friends. People frequently need rides to the grocery store or to run a few errands, so if you have a car, offer them a ride.

Once you've developed relationships with people, it is only natural to invite them to be part of the activities that you enjoy. Invite them to Campus Crusade, Bible study, an outreach, church, or a special event at church.

After you've established a comfortable relationship and gotten a good conversation on matters of faith going, you'll find people generally respond to questions of faith in one of three ways: heart, head, and holster.

Those who tend to respond with their hearts often relate to stories about personal journeys of faith, or testimonies. Everyone has a story to tell, outgoing people and shy people. Everyone can use the testimonial approach. Simply tell the story of Christ's work in your life. You don't have to have a dramatic life to have a powerful testimony. I have never heard the story of someone's journey of faith or a personal testimony that wasn't moving.

Other people come to faith on a cranial basis. They respond well to a logical and methodical approach in answering the big questions of life. If you're a person that likes thinking, logic, and grappling with the tough issues or John Calvin's Institutes, perhaps you will gravitate toward this approach with your friends.

The holster approach refers to shooting straight. Don't beat around the bush, don't sugar-coat the truth, just shoot straight. Most often I have seen this approach used by guys with other guys. I have used this approach only once — on a good female friend of mine who was systematically destroying her life by the choices she was making. The more separated people are from God by the sin in their lives, the more they need the truth in a clear and direct way. One of the best approaches to reach them is by being direct and to the point, so shoot straight.

You will probably have opportunities to use all of these approaches, but maybe you realize that you're more comfortable with one over the others. It sounds easier on paper than it really is. Having non-Christian friends can present many challenges. First off, your time with them may not be as much as with your Christian friends because you will likely choose to do different things on the weekends. You may have a friend that parties and drinks on the weekend. Or maybe you will have a friend that is promiscuous, so she wouldn't be someone you choose to go on a double date with. Sometimes you have to invest in these friends without expecting anything in return. You will be stretched, and through that stretching you will learn new ways to exhibit grace. Grace is key to building relationships and to interacting with non-Christians. A grace-filled heart is a winsome heart. A non-grace heart is cold, mean, and condescending. A grace-filled heart can be life changing to both non-Christians and Christians.

I remember sitting in class one day (supposedly working on group projects) and the girl next to me told me her testimony. She told me she used to be a cutter, and I was deeply encouraged by her story of faith. I asked this friend what it was that eventually made her become a Christian. She said it was her Christian friends. She could see a difference in them. They loved her even when she couldn't love herself. That's grace in action.

Shower all your friends with grace and mercy and you will become a contagious Christian.

FACULTY IS SINGLED OUT, TOO

Students aren't the only ones who need some grace and mercy. Christian faculty members feel the brunt of the anti-Christian hostility — and there are faculty members who are people of faith who manage to slip in under the door from time to time.

Consider University of Nebraska assistant football coach Ron Brown, widely known for being a man of faith. Brown interviewed for a coaching job at Stanford University in January 2002. Brown said he was turned down in part because of his faith in Christ and for having made statements opposing homosexuality.

The *Daily Nebraskan*, the student newspaper at the University of Nebraska, contacted Stanford and a Stanford official confirmed Brown's assertion. Several years earlier, Brown had drawn criticism from homosexual activists after stating on his Christian radio talk show, "Husker Sports Report," that "homosexuality is clearly wrong according to God's word." He also admitted to having beaten up "sissies" in grade school and feeling "hatred toward homosexuals in college — until he accepted Christ. Then, he said, he realized that "Jesus went to the Cross for the homosexual, just as He did for everyone else. It's going to take up-close intimate love of Jesus through you and me to win the homosexual to Christ.

"If I'd been discriminated against for being black, they would've never told me that," said Brown. "They had no problem telling me it was because of my Christian belief. That's amazing to me."[2]

Equally amazing is what happened to a professor at DePauw University in Greencastle, Indiana. Janis Price, a well-respected and popular elementary education instructor, put copies of *Teachers in Focus*, a publication produced by Focus on the Family, on a table in her classroom. Price did not teach from the magazines or require students read them, she simply made them available as a resource.

One of the magazines contained an article on gay activism in schools. The story, "Love Won Out," was accompanied with the text, "Feeling helpless against the onslaught of gay activists in your school? Focus on the Family has the answer for you." A student filed a complaint, and seven weeks later the professor was called to the office of Neal Abraham, the vice president of academic affairs, and told her salary was being reduced 25 percent and her job responsibilities were changing. Price's attorney, John R. Price (no relation), says Abraham told the teacher that her actions were "intolerable." The school claimed that by making the publication available, Janis Price had created a "hostile environment" for her students.

"I was absolutely amazed at that because people who know me know that I would never create a hostile environment for anyone," Janis explained.[3]

Interestingly, DePauw was founded by the United Methodist Church and still continues that relationship. The denomination's Book of Discipline states, "Homosexual persons no less than heterosexual persons are individuals of sacred worth. . . . Although we do not condone the practice of homosexuality and consider this practice incompatible with Christian teaching, we affirm that God's grace is available to all."

Price had simply offered the magazines as a resource. Attorney Price said when one student asked her about her views on homosexual teachers, she replied, "If a school hired someone to teach English or math, they need to do the best job they can at teaching English or math."

She hadn't said anything about her personal views on homosexuality. She hadn't assigned readings in the magazines, but by putting them out as a resource for students, her job was now in jeopardy.

Eventually, a Brazil, Indiana, jury determined Price' rights had been violated. She was awarded $10,401 in lost wages. She also won the case for academic freedom. At least this time.

At Indiana University, Professor Eric B. Rasmussen found himself in hot water when he added a weblog to his space on a university server and wrote that hiring a homosexual man as a schoolteacher was akin to putting the fox in the chicken coop. Rasmussen, a Yale University graduate with a doctorate from the Massachusetts Institute of Technology, specializes in game theory and arrived at IU 1992. The blog was personal, a place to record personal thoughts and the topics reflected that. They ranged from the United Nations anti-spanking position to the Disney movie *Pocahontas,* and on to showing how he velcroed a box of tissues to the ceiling of his car.[4]

Students and staff complained about Rasmussen's homosexual comments and asked that they be removed from the website. Others suggested Rasmussen, a professor of business in Indiana's Kelley School of Business, be fired. He describes himself as a conservative and a Christian who attends a nondenominational church.

Rasmussen became the center of controversy for personal thoughts he posted on a web page. Of course, if the university censors Rasmussen's speech because he is using university web servers, in the name of fairness, will they also censor thoughts posted on the Internet by students using the university servers? Other observers have wondered whether the situation will cause university offcials to limit faculty comments, even outside the classroom, that might make certain students uncomfortable.

Students aren't the only ones who feel like they're sticking their necks out from time to time. Faculty members who stick their necks out need support and encouragement. It's not like they have a large meeting akin to Campus Crusade with hundreds of fellow faculty members where they can go and recharge their batteries once a week.

Identify yourself as a Christian to a faculty member who has been open about his or her world view. Encourage them and let them know you'll be praying for them. Let them know you appreciate that they, too, are swimming against the tide.

HINDSIGHT

Feed your mind.

Don't let your professors have exclusive control over your mind. Be proactive. If you're not reading good material in class, make up for it out of class. Read the newspaper, read magazines, read books. I know it takes extra time, and college students don't always have that, but it is well worth it. Instead of just saying "I don't think that's right" in class, now you'll be able to add, "and this is why."

Debrief with friends.

When you think a professor is over the top, talk it over with a friend. Professors are entitled to opinions and you're entitled to yours, so don't keep everything pent up. You may be able to say it doesn't bother you, but day after day of hearing Christians belittled can eventually get to you. Hash it out with a friend. Tell someone what is going on. They can give you perspective, reinforce that you're not nuts, and pray for you.

Ask questions about classes/instructors.

This may be hard to do the first semester as a freshman, but spend time asking around about the reputations of professors. I have learned about certain professors that I want to avoid. Even if you find out a professor is an outspoken liberal, don't be too quick to write them off. Find out how they grade. If they are known for penalizing students who don't regurgitate their beliefs, don't waste your time. On the other hand, if a professor won't dock your grade for holding a Christian world view, as long as you can hold your own, perhaps you would like to give it a try. Keep in mind there are times you will have the energy and drive to take on a challenge and other times when you want to steer clear.

Show yourself friendly.

Be known as a cheerful Christian. It's harder for professors to be belligerent when you have a smile on your face. Show them you're confident in your beliefs by not letting *theirs* daunt your cheerfulness.

Support Christian faculty.

If you know of professors or faculty who are Christians, be sure to support them. They are in need of encouragement. They may even need it more than students do. Find a way to let them know you are a Christian, too. Many times they are as isolated as you are, if not more, because speaking up could cost them more than a grade, it could cost them a job.

Fish Out of Water

From: "Dad"

To: "Abby"

Abby,

I came across this quote from Albert Einstein and thought it might encourage you.

"Great spirits have always found violent opposition from mediocrities. The latter cannot understand it when a man does not thoughtlessly submit to hereditary prejudices but honestly and courageously uses his intelligence."

Hang in there.

Love,

Dad

From: "Nye, Abby"

To: "The Fam"

Hey, Rents,

Last night was the speech competition that all the speech classes had to attend and critique. Guess who I saw there!! Yep, the guy who wrote the article bashing Campus Crusade. I figured since I had written my letter to the editor about his piece, I should introduce myself. I went over to him when the speech competition ended, shook his hand, and struck up a conversation. I mentioned our volleys in the paper and he gave a faint smile. I asked him about his summer and post-graduation plans. He's going to Washington, D.C.! (I'm so jealous.)

It was good to talk to him. Sometimes things on paper look harsh, so it's good to be reminded that even though we are butting heads over ideology, that doesn't force us to be enemies. He seems like a pretty nice guy.

I'll actually miss having him around next year. I hope someone will step up to take his place as an outspoken liberal.

Celebrating Diversity,

Abby

*The Christian mind
has succumbed to the
secular drift with a degree of
weakness and nervelessness
unmatched in Christian history.
It is difficult to do justice in words
to the complete loss of intellectual
morale in the . . . church. One cannot
characterize it without having recourse
to language that will sound hysterical
and melodramatic. There is no
longer a Christian mind. There is
still, of course, a Christian ethic, a
Christian practice, and a Christian
spirituality. . . . But as a thinking
being, the modern Christian
has succumbed to
secularization.*

— Harry Blamires

The Party Scene

It's important to be prepared for the classroom and the situations and scenarios you may encounter, but it's also important to be prepared for campus life. There are situations and scenarios you should be prepared to encounter there as well.

For starters, there are terms you need to know as a freshman on campus. One of the most important ones may be Thirsty Thursday. Every weekend is a three-day weekend when you're at college. For many, the parties begin Thursday nights. For others, that's pure procrastination.

Dehydration appears to be a rampant health problem with college students, hence the need to drink. And drink. And drink. And drink. I'm not talking about social drinking, having a glass of wine with dinner when you're 21. I'm not even talking about the "hey, look at me I'm so cool, I'm underage, standing by a big kegger and tossing back a beer." The drinking scene has changed in recent years. It's hardened. This isn't about under-age drinkers tying one on once in a while, or once a month, but drinking continuously. Hard on the weekend, and off and on, mostly on, during the week. It's called binge drinking and college presidents agree it is the most serious problem on campus.[1]

A Harvard study found that 44 percent of U.S. college students engage in binge drinking. For females, binge drinking is described as four or more drinks in a row. For males, binge drinking is described as drinking five or more drinks in a row. Forty percent of college women are binge drinkers and 51 percent of the men are binge drinkers. Binge drinkers are typically white, age 23 or younger, and residents of a fraternity or sorority.[2] If you binge in high school, you're likely to binge in college. Finally, the study found binge drinkers binge three or more times in a two-week period.

Actually, the risks associated with alcohol abuse have been documented and are rather wide-ranging. A study by Bell and Howell Information and Learning found:

- Binging and intoxication decrease GPA directly and indirectly by reducing study hours.

- College drinking increases the probability of choosing a business major, but decreases the probability of choosing engineering.

- The effects of heavy drinking on GPA and major choice reduce future weekly earnings by between 0.3 and 9.8 percent.[3]

On paper, statistics are cold, hard, boring numbers, but when you go to college and the statistics have faces, it's another matter. The hurt brought about by alcohol abuse can be fleeting and temporary (a hangover), or long lasting and deadly.

The statistics became personal and heart wrenching at Ball State University in Muncie, Indiana, in 2003. A 21-year-old student named Michael S. McKinney had been out drinking when he decided to return to the house he was staying at around 3:30 a.m. Disoriented and intoxicated, McKinney went to the wrong house and began pounding on the back door. The homeowner, panicked and frightened, called police and reported that someone was trying to break into her house.

A Ball State University police officer, 24, and fairly new on the job, arrived on the scene and repeatedly yelled at the young man to "Stop! Get down!" Neighbors were watching from their windows, as the homeowner had called them to alert them to the situation. They watched as the officer yelled. They watched as McKinney lunged at the officer and the officer fired his gun four times, killing the student.

Tragic. Absolutely tragic. In a split second, lives changed forever. Grief sent shock waves in a thousand different directions. It took investigators weeks to sort out the facts of the Ball State tragedy, but one fact that was clear from the beginning: When you engage in activities that dull your senses and numb your brain, you put yourself at risk.

GREEK TO ME

True to the stereotype, Greek houses are often the hot spots for drinking and accompanying rowdiness. I went to a frat party the first week of college to see what it was like. My friends and I walked all throughout the house, in part because we got turned around. (I can't imagine trying to find my way out if I were drunk.) Everyone was drinking. In the basement there was laughter and cheering as the guys were playing a chugging drinking game. There was dancing and smoking in other parts of the house, but for the most part, the entire party consisted of boozing, boozing, and more boozing. It was dull, so we decided to leave. I was surprised at how boring the party actually was, plus the majority of them probably ended up puking that night, followed by a hangover the next morning and no memory of what they did. And this is fun? A lot of what passes for fun is due to boredom. Mix that with a lot of affluence and shortage of imagination and you have party after party, the same ol', same ol'.

Of course, it would be grossly unfair to paint every fraternity member with the same brush. Not every member is a hard-drinking party animal. A friend I met at a student leadership forum on faith and values lives in a fraternity hall and does not fit the stereotype at all. He doesn't drink and he doesn't party. He hopes by being a member of a fraternity that he'll have an influence and make a difference. He wishes that more Christians would join fraternities to help broaden their influence. When the frat house has party nights he goes up to his room and shuts the door or leaves. Of course, he still has clean-up duty the next day. Obviously, he doesn't have much of a direct influence on party nights, but maybe on other days of the week he's building relationships with guys in his house, hoping they can see a difference in him and his actions.

He's deliberately put himself in a difficult position. The first time he slips up in anything — and anybody who is human slips up at something — he comes under a critical gaze. Because he's chosen to be different, people are continually watching him and, in many cases, waiting for him to blow it.

Sadly, a number of students who engage in under-age drinking and excessive drinking are professing Christians. There is a major disconnect in the minds of many Christians today. They've bought into the cliché that it's easier to ask for forgiveness than permission. It's all about rationalizing. Drink yourself under the table on Friday and Saturday, ask for forgiveness at church on Sunday. That's what Dietrich Bonheoffer called cheap grace.

If we profess the faith, we need to live it with our lives, our words, our actions, and our attitudes. There has to be a connection between what we believe and how we live.

There are things to do and ways to have fun that don't require alcohol. Fortunately, I was lucky enough to plug into a small group that shared my ideas. We don't drink ourselves into oblivion or go to frat parties. We don't even bum around and watch movies much. We check out what's going on in the city and often leave campus on Friday and Saturday nights.

Big cities have a lot to offer in regard to restaurants, shows, malls, and museums. Sometimes we get dressed up and go to a restaurant, or we go ice skating, to the art museum, or take a walk downtown. Pedal boating downtown on the canal and watching movies outside on the wall of the art museum are specialties we enjoy. Other times, we do a drive-and-search for a new hangout, or pick a hole-in-the-wall to frequent for a while. We ride bikes, go on picnics, and have served dinner at the city mission. We go to the grocery store and make dinner together, connect with families who live near campus, and have even gone home for the weekend to hang with one another's families. We read books, discuss them, and when we're feeling extremely strange, have been known to play a card game in a foreign language. There are all kinds of ways to let down and even be crazy, ways that don't involve drinking until you puke.

A significant number of students, Christians and non-Christians, are pulling away from the booze model of college life. It's actually part of an emerging trend.

The recent Harvard University School of Public Health College Alcohol Study that surveyed students at 119 colleges noted a trend toward polarization of students since 1993. Students are either abstaining completely from alcohol or frequently binge drinking. Each category increased by about one-fifth, with abstainers increasing from 16.4 percent to 19.3 percent (and frequent binge drinkers increasing from 19.7 to 22.8 percent of the college population).

For every group of frequent binge drinkers, remember somewhere on campus there are an equal number of students who aren't tipping back at all. The challenge is to find them.

At the beginning of the year, students often introduce themselves and identify themselves as a partier or a non-partier. They'll tell you straight out.

"What do you like to do? On the weekend?"

The answer is usually either, "I like to party," or a brief hesitation and "I'm not really into the parties." Speak up. Don't hesitate to identify yourself as someone who can have fun without a bottle in each hand. Be bold right away, because the first of the year is when everyone is making connections. Sometimes finding this group is slow going. Sometimes it's so slow going, it's downright depressing. You wonder if you'll ever connect. Don't give up. Keep looking.

Look at who's walking through the dorm hall on a Friday or Saturday night. The fact that they *aren't* at a frat party is an indicator they may be someone who knows how to have a good time without getting drunk or hooking up.

The non-partiers are on campus. They're there in growing numbers. There are people with imagination and creativity, students who don't blindly follow the keg, waiting to have fun, too. You just have to look. Looking shouldn't be too hard. Since you haven't been drinking, your vision won't be blurred.

THE REST OF THE PARTY

Drinking and keggers are one-half of the party scene. The other half is the sex. Everybody knows pre-marital sex is part of college life, but what you might not know is just how open people are about it. Or how raunchy, or tawdry, or how proud they are of it.

A marker board on the door of a room in my hall summed up the attitude of many college students very nicely: "All I want to do is get drunk and get laid." Other marker boards resounded the same theme using even more vulgarities and even coarser language.

A guy friend in my hall said he wanted me to meet his girlfriend when she came for the weekend. We had developed a friendship, so I knew he could handle straight talk. I asked him where she would be staying. He said she would stay in his room. I said, "Oh, well, she's more than welcome to stay in my room, I can sleep in a sleeping bag and she can have my bed." He just smiled. So did I.

When his girlfriend came to visit, the message on his marker board, said, "Knock first." I guess the girlfriend, still a senior in high school, didn't want to stay in my room. She preferred sleeping in a top bunk with her boyfriend and sharing a bathroom with four guys, three of whom she'd never met before. Having someone of the opposite sex share your bed, and even having sex with them while your roommate is in the room does not even raise an eyebrow anymore.

By the end of the weekend, my friend's roommate was ready to see the girl go. He complained that she took too long in the bathroom. But he was also irritated because she kept walking around in her underwear. You have to wonder where the sense of privacy, or even embarrassment, went. And to think that back in grade school we wore shorts under our dresses on the playground to protect our privacy during recess. Something's wrong when an 8 year old has a more finely tuned sense of modesty than an 18 year old.

The pressure to look skanky and act sleazy at college is intense. Even the girls that don't sleep around try to keep up appearances that hint that they are at least amenable to the idea. Today, there's little a female can do, or wear, on campus that will shock anyone. As a matter of fact, it is as if a girl can damage her reputation if someone thinks she actually has standards, morals, and convictions.

Truthfully, it's not hard to figure out why even good girls want to look bad. Good girls want to look bad because girls who dress modestly are overlooked. Most guys don't pay attention to modestly clothed girls, at least not when there is another girl ten feet away wearing low-cut pants and a low-cut shirt and has cleavage on display. Here's a hard truth females have to learn to live with if you go to college and maintain any standard of modesty and purity: When you dress modestly you become nearly invisible.

I told that to a woman in her forties and the woman said, "Those type guys aren't worth having. They grow up to be men who pick up trophy wives the minute their own wives start to wrinkle or sag. You don't want that kind of guy now and you won't want him later. Wait for a guy who appreciates a gal who's modest."

Nearly all forms of modesty have virtually disappeared. My parents were dropping me off on campus after the Thanksgiving break. They pulled over on the main drag that rings the campus where a number of others kids were being shuttled back to campus, duffle bags and laptops all deposited curbside.

Fish Out of Water

A couple was walking down the sidewalk toward the line of cars pulled over dropping off students. The guy had his arm around the girls shoulder, they were smiling and talking. All of a sudden he dropped his hand down and grabbed her breast. Is she going to smack him? Will she stop in her tracks, shocked? Will she turn the other direction and leave him in her dust? No. She grabbed him in a rather sensitive place. They continue walking a few steps with good grips on parts of one another that were once considered extremely private.

The concept of shame has been so perverted that possessing a sense of shame is now something for which a young woman is made to feel ashamed. This is well illustrated by a column that appeared in the campus newspaper. The piece addresses the "Walk of Shame," that lengthy trek a disheveled girl makes as she walks back to her dorm after a one-night stand at a frat house or boy's dorm. It is not uncommon to see a girl on a walk of shame early Saturday or Sunday mornings. Many times these girls are wearing someone else's clothes, looking tired, and even embarrassed as they quickly walk back to their own room.

The walk is usually made with head down and a posture of shame. No more. She's been set free according to this writer, a business major, who wrote the following for the student newspaper.

WALK OF SHAME

Wake up early on any Friday, Saturday, or Sunday morning here . . . and you are likely to see an indicator of the wildness of the night before. If you're lucky, a look out the window or a short drive down Hampton will reveal one embarrassed, exhausted girl who was the company of one lucky guy the night before. She's on her way home. She's hoping that everyone will still be asleep and that she'll make it to her destination unnoticed. We have labeled this stroll the "Walk of Shame."

If it were up to me, people wouldn't look at this little girl (wearing baggy clothes that obviously don't belong to her) with such disgrace.

Everyone is aware of the circumstances and we all know the situation. Perhaps you've been in this girl's sneakers and you know precisely how she feels. Anyway, it's quite clear that if you are up and at 'em at this hour, early enough to catch this young lady on her stroll, it means she had a much better time than you did last night. You were in your room studying for a test or writing a paper while she was living it up like any normal, fun-loving, beer-drinking college student would do. After all, that's why we came to college, isn't it?

So, I propose a change in thinking. . . . I suggest that this walk not be judged or teased in any way. Instead, go back home and look in the mirror and cry, because you are wasting the most fun time of your life.

The cute little girl should be commended for her party personality and you are the one that should be scolded.

Congratulations, you're a nerd.[4]

Twice the student columnist referenced this type of female in the Walk of Shame as a "little girl." I wonder if the writer refers to himself and his guy friends as "little boys?" His tone reveals his lack of respect for a young woman's modesty, privacy, and dignity. If the Walk of Shame is as commonplace as the writer suggests it is, doesn't he for a moment wonder exactly what is it that makes these young ladies feel embarrassed and empty deep down inside?

Most girls who have been in that position, no matter what they may say or the bravado they may muster, still feel dirty and used deep down. I've talked to some of the girls. There is often an emptiness and a longing inside. So they move to the next one and the next one and the next one, hoping to find the connection that truly connects.

A must read for any young woman heading to college is Wendy Shalit's book, *A Return to Modesty: Discovering the Lost Virtue*. Shalit offers a deeper understanding of modesty. She traces the link between the lack of modesty and immorality. She also offers strong documentation on the ugly fallout of immodesty and immorality — eating disorders, emotional problems, the traumatic fallout that follows abortions, lack of self-confidence, anxiety, and depression. Shalit builds a case that modesty is actually a form of power. Modesty is a powerful form of control that females have at their disposal. Yet, so many females yield that power so easily, and with so little thought.

Shalit's book was written while she, too, was at college, so her experience is fresh and her insights unique. She concludes her in-depth analysis of modesty and immodesty with an interesting thought: "Modesty is proof that morality is sexy. It may even be the proof of God, because it means that we have been designed in such a way that when we humans act like animals, without any restraint and without any rules, we just don't have as much fun"[5]

Shalit cites a Jewish proverb: *Ein b'not yisrael hefker*. Translation: "The daughters of Israel are not for public use." When you look around most college campuses today, it would appear that the daughters of America *are* for public use. It would appear they are available for public use by both the way they dress and by the way they behave.

HOOKING UP

Pia Nordlinger, writing for the *Women's Quarterly*, published by the Independent Women's Forum, says college these days is all about "hooking up." The "relationship" usually ends when the girl tiptoes out the door the next morning.

Nordlinger writes, "When it comes to sex, a young man entering college today has it made: He won't have to shell out for flowers, a pricey dinner, or a sappy chick flick. He won't even have to call her the next day. Guess who won the Sexual Revolution?

"Although girls defend the practice of hooking up, they sense that they are getting shortchanged. They know that the status quo — going to bars, drinking too much, and following a guy home to bed — is somehow detrimental. The problem for them is that they are both unwilling and unable to articulate why."[6]

In 1997, a *Details* magazine "Sex on Campus" survey revealed that almost one-third of college women had "sex with someone they didn't even like." Why? "It just happened," was the common response.

The message on campus is that if you're not hooking up and sleeping around, you're a boring prude. When I'm surrounded by that mindset, there are times when I start to wonder if I'm missing out on something. But deep down I know I'm not missing out, I'm waiting for something more — more intimacy, more commitment, more permanence.

Sex, in the bounds of marriage, is best because that is how God intended it. The oneness in marriage comes from an intimacy built upon vulnerability. This vulnerability is fragile and it needs to be protected. That's why it's self-destructive to go around exposing our hearts and emotions at random. Vulnerability is not cheap, or easy to come by, like the free key chains and frisbees they give away under the welcome tent the first week of school. Sex is the ultimate expression of vulnerability.

Marriage is worth waiting for and the reasons are many.

Adults who engaged in sex outside marriage express less sexual satisfaction than do married couples.

Married people express greater physical pleasure and emotional satisfaction from sex than do unmarried people.

People who live together or were unmarried and having sex are more likely than married men and women to say that sex made them feel anxious, worried, afraid, or guilty.

PARTY RESPONSIBLY

At the Campus Crusade meeting the week before spring break, the guys and gals were split up into separate groups. The message was, "Don't have sex during spring break." It was an attempt to combat all the material that had been floating around for the previous two weeks. Different campus-sponsored organizations had passed out flyers on how to party responsibly, which means "use a condom." Then spring break goodie bags were passed out, which contained condoms.

It's commendable that Campus Crusade attempted to present the opposing view, but much of the message passed overhead. It's not enough to say "don't have sex" (although it probably should be — God makes it pretty simple), it seems we need to explain why. Students, yes, Christian students, need to understand that God's rules have an individual's best interest at heart. Every Christian student needs to know *why* he or she shouldn't have sex before marriage. If you don't know why before you come to campus, you're sure not going to learn why once you're here. It's an understanding you better bring with you when you come.

Joshua Harris, author of *I Kissed Dating Goodbye*, says, "Physical intimacy is much more than two bodies colliding. God designed our sexuality as a physical expression of the oneness of marriage. God guards it carefully and places many stipulations on it because He considers it extremely precious. A man and woman who commit their lives to each other in marriage gain the right to express themselves sexually to each other. A husband and wife may enjoy each other's bodies because they in essence belong to each other. But if you're not married to someone, you have no claim on that person's body, no right to sexual intimacy."[7]

Sex is so casual on campuses today that it is often compared to having all the significance of scratching someone's back. There's a whole lot of scratching going on today.

If you live out your Christian convictions, there will be times when you feel like you're the only one not "scratching."

At those times, I remind myself that I know the kind of life I want and I've made a commitment to make it happen. With God's grace I can reach that goal. Romans 12:2 says, "Do not be conformed to this world but be transformed by the renewing of your mind." God does not want us to conform to the promiscuity around us. We are to stand apart from the crowd. Contentment in choosing abstinence comes from the understanding that you are not missing out by not sleeping around, but rather you will experience more fulfilling sex in marriage, sexuality the way it was intended.

Sadly, many of those who sleep around often wake up to the reality that they are hurting themselves — emotionally, physically, and spiritually — and setting themselves up for a life of pain and regret. Harris says, "God's love for the impure does not cease, but their ability to enjoy this love does." If you've already been caught up in the crowd, if you've made mistakes, or if this is a new and appealing concept to you, it is never too late to change. There is absolutely nothing too big for God to forgive. God's power can work in you to transform your mind, body, and soul. The Christian life is about new beginnings and fresh starts, so why wait? Recommit to Christ and His biblical plan for sexuality.

HINDSIGHT

If you love me

There's an incredible disconnect among Christian students on secular campuses today. You see certain students at Campus Crusade meetings on a weekday night and then you see the same students talking about getting drunk on the weekend. It's far more offensive and hypocritical for someone who claims to be a Christian to be engaged in such behavior than for someone who never claims to be a Christian in the first place. It's an easy slide down — the pressure is tremendous — but it's a slide Christians are not to make. John 14:15 says, "If you love me you will obey what I command."

To party or not to party

Some students say they're comfortable at parties where there is under-age drinking. That may be so, but remember this: under-age drinking is illegal. More and more campuses are enforcing the law and handing out penalties.

Need a ride?

On a secular campus, you're bound to have friends who drink and drink to get drunk. Let them know it's not your thing, but also let them know if they're ever in a jam and need help getting home, they can give you a call.

Play it straight

Try not to be too repulsed by what you see around you. Work at keeping a poker face. You never know when there may be an opportunity to reach someone.

Be there for the breakdown

As a Christian, you can't condone sleeping around, but you don't have to be condescending to others either. Just be there. Be there for them when they hurt. Be a friend. Listen, comfort, and when the time is right, point them in a different direction. Point them in the direction that says self-control is a good thing. Point them in the direction that says human beings are too vulnerable and complex to engage in sex on such a casual basis. Point them in the direction that says the Creator has mandated that sex is to be reserved for a most holy and intimate union.

Not everybody

There will be times when you feel like you're the only one not hooking up on campus. You're not the only one *not* doing it and not everybody *is* doing it. But what if that was the case? So what? Would it matter? God calls us to do the difficult.

Porn

Pornography is nearly inescapable on a college campus. Especially for guys. It's a big pastime in the dorms and in the frat houses. Statistics say that now more females are viewing porn for entertainment as well. Even if you don't view, it's bound to come up in conversation. It can be a great opportunity for discussion. You can simply say, "I'm not into that," or you can use it as a door into a deeper discussion. "I'm not into that. I think it's disrespectful to women and men and trivializes sexuality."

You've Got Mail

From: "Katie"

To: "Abby"

As a freshman I found myself in a whirlwind of drinking, partying, stealing, sex, and everything in between, and this after having been on staff with my youth group not a week earlier. To make matters even worse was the fact I was on the water polo team that was highly regarded on the Division I level and automatic friends with teammates that were older than me and far less moral.

The bottom line is this . . . I went on to be an All-American in my sport, as well as an academic All-American, all while harboring alcoholism and depression. After almost swindling my God-given talent on every enticement of the world, I cried out to God and He answered me. I took a year off and allowed God to build in me a firm foundation that could weather the storms that are now being thrown at me. After a year of Discipleship Training School, missions, and running youth camps, I moved back to school a week ago to see the same deceptions you are warning incoming freshmen of.

God has already been able to use me in incredible ways, plus He has given me the opportunity to play water polo again. God has put it into my heart to reach out to the troubled and lost of our generation and show them that there is hope and freedom in the Lord — apart from the accepted norm of drugs, sex, and violence.

Katie

Having
taught at two
public universities and
two public community colleges,
including currently teaching full-time
at a public community college, I can
completely identify with Abby Nye Suddarth's
thesis in her excellent book, Fish Out of Water.
She is exactly correct in her contention that
our nation's public colleges are indoctrinating
students into moral relativism. Although
critical thinking is given much lip service by
professors, she rightly points out in this book
that "groupthink" is actually what is being
encouraged and that the highest virtue is
"tolerance" — of anything except conservative
Christianity, which is viewed as being
intolerant. The goal of higher education now
seems to be conforming students' thinking
to the politically correct ideology of moral
relativism under the guise of promoting
"diversity."

Steve Wolfe, M.A.
Founder of Creation Education Ministries

Posters and Pin-ups

When you consider that everyone in my generation who has attended public school has been fed a steady diet of sex education, substance abuse warnings, and diatribes on the evils of tobacco since second grade, you might think it would be safe to assume this group of young people had mastered the nuts and bolts of such relatively simple topics. Apparently not. Judging from the posters that pop up on the walls of campus buildings, we are in dire need of immediate and in-depth remedial education.

What's the big deal about posters? In one sense, they're not a big deal, but in another sense they are. Sure, they're just pictures with slogans, but those pictures with slogans have a cumulative effect. They constantly, steadily, quietly promote an immoral lifestyle. It is a rear attack on morality. The attack may be a silent one, but it is a successful one in that it often has the end result of desensitizing viewers to morality and absolute truth. Week after week, the posters portray a message which eventually wears on one's conscience. The posters paint a picture of the abnormal being normal and of sin being attractive, fun, hip, consequence-free, and desirable.

The first poster that caught my eye as a freshman was right around the corner from my dorm room. I saw it as I was moving in boxes.

ONE OUT OF THREE AMERICANS DON'T DRINK — AND THAT'S OKAY, TOO.

The poster seems relatively benign but there is an element to the message that is condescending. First, it points out that if you don't drink, you're in the minority. It may not be intended, but the tone of the poster suggests that you're out of the loop if you don't drink, but try not to worry about being out of the loop. And odd. And in the minority.

A lot of money, time, and effort go into the posters that publicize weird programs and events. The strange thing to me is that a lot of these programs and posters are created by adults in their 40s and 50s, people you'd expect to have some degree of maturity or decorum.

Sexual Assault Awareness Week kicked off soon after classes started with a poster blitz featuring a photograph of an attractive young couple with their heads nestled together. They were looking at the camera with that forlorn "I'm-so-misunderstood" look that is popular among models today. The copy on the poster read:

My strength is not for hurting.
So when I wanted to and she didn't, we didn't.
MEN CAN STOP RAPE
Respect, equality & peace.
Everybody's got a right.

Well, that's what the poster said for a couple of days until someone took a felt tip pen and made an addition. The poster then read:

MEN CAN STOP RAPE
so can mace and a 9 millimeter

Another poster that made a debut was a bright blue number with a red stop sign in the center and big yellow parentheses on the right and left sides. The text said:

((RESPECT THE BOUNDARIES))

A good message, but somewhat contradictory to every other message on campus that says we shouldn't have to live by boundaries, as that would be restricting freedom. Respect the boundaries in relationships, but don't respect them anywhere else?

Sexual Assault Prevention Week was followed by more sexual activity, or non-activity, depending on your boundaries, as we commenced with the Battles of the Sexes.

Meet with a bunch of Guys & Girls
to ask them questions about
SEX
college life, dating,
and anything else you can think of
FREE FOOD

No mention of Jerry Springer, but you had the feeling if he had stopped by, he would have fit right in. After Labor Day and before Columbus Day, the campus celebrated National Coming Out Day. Cafeteria tables were adorned with bright orange flyers listing famous people who had come out of the closet and explained that the first step of coming out is "coming out to yourself."

This coincided with a lecture put on by the campus Alliance on "What the Bible REALLY says about Homosexuality."

As the Thanksgiving and Christmas holidays approached, the campus was blanketed with pamphlets and flyers about a lot of drinking awareness programs. (Again, the underlying assumption is that everybody does, so if you don't, what does that say about you?) The Alcohol Self-Test pamphlet, widely circulated, tested the reader's knowledge about alcohol, with brain teasers like:

Alcohol slows down your reaction time.
True ____ False ____

The checklist on "How Safely Do I Drink" offered these:

I never drink on an empty stomach
Yes____ No____
I don't gulp my drinks
Yes ____ No____
If I am taking any prescription drugs I don't drink
Yes ____ No ____

A couple of days later, "Getting What You Want from Drinking" was distributed at every cafeteria table. It was an informative pamphlet on how to drink more safely, how to avoid weight gain, along with information on hangovers and morning-after crashes. Again, these messages are like the nagging wife compared to a dripping faucet in Proverbs. The steady beat of the assumption is that everybody gets rip-roaring drunk, therefore, if you don't, what does that say about you? Curiously, despite the fact that most freshmen and sophomores on campus would be under age, there was never any mention of the risks of being busted for under-age drinking and the consequences likely to follow.

Also in December came a special event complete with accompanying posters featuring Rebekka Armstrong. Armstrong was featured in a program called EXPOSED that tours college campuses. Armstrong, by way of background, is a young woman who "aspired to become a Playboy Playmate at 18." One can only assume things didn't go well with the SATs. The poster continues: "Against all odds, she was chosen out of hundreds of thousands of young women to become a centerfold. Miss September '86 became an immediate fixture in the star-studded world of Hollywood."

Hollywood brought Armstrong a lot of new experiences, including becoming HIV positive. No other female speaker on campus had the poster play that the former Playboy Playmate did. That's a rather sad commentary. When you think of all the women of no-table achievement, women of truly great accomplishment, women who have used their brains and talents to advance not only them-selves but other people, it's ironic that the campus chose to invite and heavily publicize an event by a former Playboy bunny.

The poster promoting the former bunny's appearance had a pic-ture of Armstrong in a Playboy bunny shirt and low-slung jeans, with another photo inset in the lower corner. In the inset photo, Armstrong was buck naked, playing coy with the camera, hooked up to an IV. As if being HIV positive could somehow look sexy and attractive.

Again, a poster subtly and silently promotes immorality as the new morality. It was no great shock that Armstrong's appearance was made possible by the Playboy Foundation. The irony here is not to be missed. The most exploitive, anti-woman, the-chick-is-nothing-but-a-sex-object corporation in the history of the nation is producing a program to alert the uninformed about the possibility of contracting HIV! Whatever. And I don't say whatever lightly. I say whatever because the college Alliance group is fond of saying it. It's a new sexual identification group.

The Alliance is continually putting up posters advertising week-ly meetings for those with different sexual orientations. Because this is a campus that promotes diversity, the poster says:

Gay. Straight. Whatever.

And, in case you were unaware, Crossdressing Day is celebrated February 1.

Show off your costume in the Dawg pound!
Prizes will be awarded for best dressed.

From the looks of the poster, short skirts, thigh-high socks, and midriff shirts were in. So was heavy make-up, blue eye shadow, and bee-stung lips. Crossdressers must not have gotten the memo that the natural look is back. Less is more.

February is a big month for "special activities," as it coincides with Valentine's Day. Valentine's Day has been so dragged through the mud, a lot of students would rather skip it and head directly to April Fool's Day.

Relationship Week is observed in the middle of February. There are a variety of activities and plays throughout Relationship Week, all of which culminate in National Condom Day on February 14 when free condoms are given away in the cafeteria. (What? You're *not* having pre-marital sex, hooking up on weekends? What's wrong with you?)

Relationship Week, ad nauseum, yielded an abundance of posters and flyers including a hot pink number featuring the following:

Tips for Guys to Make a Relationship Work

1. Don't Lie About the Important Stuff

Don't lie about important things. No good can come from saying you come from a rich family when in fact you don't, or claiming you're a subdued intellectual when in fact you prefer beer and football to talking about Tolstoy, any day. *[Good advice. Lying is never conducive to healthy relationships.]*

2. Don't Start Criticizing Your Partner

Some say there is no right time to express your opinion negatively when a relationship starts, but if you feel a strong need to do so, make your comment a mere suggestion and not an insult. Instead of "That dress is ugly," say "I preferred the beautiful black one you wore on New Year's Eve." *[I only hope these people aren't interpersonal communication majors.]*

3. Don't Meet the Parents

Although you love your parents and quirky Uncle Bob, it is best to introduce your family at a time when she'll easily understands [*sic*] your motives and is able to put up with some uncomfortable questions from a rude grandfather. *[Who's rude?]*

4. Don't Focus on Sex

It is important that you show them that sex need not come first. If you want to make this relationship a serious one, don't think of sex as a top priority. This is a great move on your part, as you are showing your special someone how smitten you are with their mind. *[The message here is that obviously you want pre-marital sex and will get pre-marital sex, but to do so, it's best to be manipulative about it. The strategy on being impressed with the other person's mind will probably work as long as they don't try talking about Kierkegaard.]*

National Condom Day was followed by a campus-sponsored activity called "Just How Kinky Are You?" Here we are, scholars in the making (at least in my rich fantasy world) and the university sponsors an event plumbing the depths of kinky. This hot pink poster featured:

Dirty Minds
The Game of Naughty Clues
Sexy Games and Dirty Minds

The posters and special weeks start winding down in the spring with the exception of spring break, which is the last big hurrah. The Counseling and Consultation Center — a place you'd think would be staffed by health professionals knowing something about STDs and the micro-organisms that can pass through condoms, and might even occasionally think about morality, ethics, and emotional well being — began distributing spring break flyers titled:

Road Trip?

The flyer included instructions on how to

PARTY TO LIVE!

This flyer detailed what to pack for spring break — condoms, sunscreen, and condoms — and even offered a technique for "enhancing sensation." You have to wonder how that conversation went in the counseling office. Then again, it's probably best not to. Ever the voice of reason, the flyer also admonished students to set a drinking plan and what to do in case a drinking buddy:

> . . . can't be roused by shaking or shouting, has shallow, irregular slowed respiration, has cold, clammy pale bluish skin, took downers with alcohol, is severely disoriented or anxious, sustained a blow to the head, has a bleeding injury, or drank way more than their usual amount.

The flyer continued:

> Now, a few words about GHB. GHB is made on the street. Yeah, so what? You never really know what's in it or how potent it is. When combined with alcohol, GHB can be even more deadly (among other things you can STOP BREATHING).

Don't say they didn't warn you. Don't say they didn't tell you that deadly means to stop breathing. Don't say they didn't spell it out.

Essentially, the pre-spring break message was get out there, drink, party down, and try not to kill yourself. Hey, and be safe! Okay? And above all, KEEP BREATHING!

SEX IN THE LOUNGE?

A friend at the University of Pittsburgh was very confused by a message she saw posted on the dorm's official message board. The message said, "Sex in the lounge — 9 p.m." She asked a dorm-mate if she thought there actually was going to be sex in the lounge. Her friend looked at the sign and laughed, realizing the message board was inviting people to watch "Sex in the City," in the lounge. The point is, the campus atmosphere is sometimes so raunchy that sex in the lounge is believable.

People will respond differently to the barrage of tacky posters advertising events on campus. Some people are oblivious to the posters. Others detach themselves and laugh at them. Personally, I was discouraged being bombarded with their ridiculous messages. For the first few weeks, it was another wave in the blast of culture shock. I realized most of the posters aren't created by students, although some do come from students with an agenda. Others apparently come from very frustrated middle-aged people at the counseling center. There's really not much that can be done about the posters. If they are vulgar, you can complain to your Resident Assistant (but they have strict orders to display every poster). Those who are deeply offended sometimes take the posters down themselves.

After some gay posters were plastered all over campus, one had been taken down off a bulletin board outside one of my classrooms. I noticed that the missing poster was soon replaced by a terse note from the Gay/Straight Alliance saying that it was a hate crime to take down their poster. If you're contemplating the idea of taking the posters down yourself, use your judgment, or at least know what the punishment is at your school if you get caught.

Keep your eyes open and your mind sharp when you're bombarded with a deluge of immoral messages from posters in the hall. Think about what they are really saying. The accumulative impact of these posters can be significant. Don't fall for the lie that an immoral lifestyle is normal or desirable. There are people out there who can tell you otherwise; they just haven't made it to the posters in the hall yet.

HINDSIGHT

Remind yourself

Whether you're the type to take the posters as blaring personal insults, or the type that generally doesn't notice the tacky poster until a friend draws attention to it three weeks after it's been on the wall, it is hard to ignore them forever. As insignificant as it may seem at the time, these subtle visuals have a cumulative effect — the effect is disheartening. And what is even more disheartening is that there is not much that can be done about it. Cognitively, the best thing to do is distance yourself from the messages. The messages on the posters may be reality for some people, but remind yourself, they're definitely not reality for all people.

You've Got Mail

From: "Jeremy"

To: "Abby"

Subject: revolution

I think for me it was difficult to connect. I wasn't real motivated my freshman year when I went away and was discouraged by the things going on around me on campus and in the dorms. i connected with an on-campus church, the revolution. it was oriented toward the college crowd and was real good about getting students introduced to other students and helping to plug them in no only with their peers but also with people of authority in the church to help ground us and create different levels of accountability. sometimes it felt like the church groups were more like social groups, but that could have been a reflection of a poor attitude on my part. i looked at one or two other groups on campus, not too many, and they seemed to lack much depth which turned me off to them.

later,

j

A question that
needs to be answered
is "why are so many
professors so hostile toward
Christianity?" Part of the answer
is, in my experience, most of the text
books (and thus the professors in college,
as their information comes largely from the
textbooks) are very biased against Christianity.
The professors are not trying to be cruel, but
genuinely believe that Christianity has been, as
a whole, a force for evil in history. I can remember
only a couple of favorable references to Christianity
in college (and I had a minor in history). All of the rest
were very negative and influenced me, as an adult,
to become an atheist. It was only when I explored
the anti-Christian allegations, such as the crusades
and the Galileo affair, that I learned the full story. It
was then I realized that I had been badly mislead
in college. The information I later learned is
available to those who dig into these events
and read widely, but is not commonly found
in textbooks or college lectures. The facts
about Galileo are widely known among
Galileo scholars, but this information
rarely works its way down to the
common people and into the
textbooks.

— Jerry Bergman, Ph.D.

CHAPTER 9

Survive and Thrive

I f you choose to attend a secular college or university, know that your survival will require action. Demands it. You cannot expect to quietly sit through four years of liberal propaganda that often openly attacks your Christian faith without being influenced. Survival is important. But it might also be that God wants you to do more than learn to cope with the situation. If you decide to go to a secular school, determine right now to do more than just survive on the sidelines. Determine to thrive — to join the action, engage in debate, and be part of the discussion.

If you'd asked me if I considered myself a conservative when I started college, I would have said yes. If you asked me if I was a staunch conservative or a radical conservative, I would have said no. But then something happened. As the days and weeks passed and I heard the leaders and heroes I had long looked up to bashed, trashed, and disrespected, and as I heard my faith mocked and ridiculed, I realized something. It wasn't enough to hold my own or play defense in this environment. To survive here, I'd have to play offense. I couldn't worry about what people thought about me; the call was to be energized and sometimes even outspoken. Polite and friendly, but outspoken. It was the only way to survive and thrive in the muck of liberal ideology and moral relativism.

Dinesh D'Souza explains this shift in thinking far better than I could. "Typically, the conservative attempts to conserve, to hold onto the values of the existing society. But what if the existing society is liberal? What if the existing society is inherently hostile to conservative beliefs? It is foolish for a conservative to attempt to conserve that culture. Rather, he must seek to undermine it, to thwart it, to destroy it at the root level. This means that the conservative must stop being conservative. More precisely, he must be philosophically conservative but temperamentally radical."

For a Christian, this call to be radical must be tempered with respect and love. But don't think that respect and love translate into some sort of passivity. The society that exists on campus is liberal, *very liberal*, especially in the soft science departments where personal opinion and subjectivity so easily make their way into the classroom. To survive in this type of society, you have to speak up and articulate your beliefs. Boldly. When professors push lies, offer the truth. When campus activities are offensive, voice your complaints. When the campus newspaper prints some whacked-out article trumping the joys of binge drinking or group sex, write a letter to the editor.

You're squirming here, aren't you? Sounding a little hard-edged for a Christian? Don't forget, Paul fully exercised his rights as a Roman citizen when it was to his advantage. Jesus was a powerhouse when He encountered the enemies of God. He used language describing excrement and filth. He used the language of tombs, snakes, and thieves and robbers who wore the masks of self-righteousness. David Mills, in *Recovering the Art of Christian Polemics,* points out that Polycarp, one of the saints of the early church, didn't mince words when referring to Marcion, the heretic. He called him "the firstborn of Satan." Irenaeus thought Marcion was one who "spoke with the mouth of the devil."[1]

Now, it would hardly be effective or beneficial to march into the classroom with a professor who enjoys bashing Christianity and start calling him the firstborn of Satan or drawing analogies to excrement. I am saying that we need to rekindle the fire. There's complacency about many of us today. We need to fuel the passion for truth. Words mean things and ideas are worth discussing.

Yes, we should live peaceably with all men. But living peaceably is not the equivalent of living in silent surrender and waving the white flag. And yes, we should speak the truth in love. But speaking the truth in love doesn't always mean whispering. I've witnessed my parents speaking the truth in love to the three of us kids at different times and believe me, sometimes their voices have been very loud. Sometimes their noses were only a few inches away from ours.

Sometimes, speaking the truth in love, and loving aggressively, demands a high energy. We don't have much of that passion today. We've grown tepid. Our salt is losing its saltiness and our light is flickering on a weak set of AA batteries. It's time to rekindle the flame. Opportunities abound.

On the first day of philosophy class, my professor, who had a reputation as a hard-core liberal feminist known for lively class discussions, told us that if she ever says anything offensive, we were more than welcome to come talk to her about it. Take advantage of opportunities like those! The professor then went on to cuss like a sailor, salting her sentences with G - d- - -. I ignore the bulk of cussing that goes on around me, but G - d - - is extremely offensive to me as a Christian.

I took her up on her offer and met with her after class. I politely explained how I was looking forward to her class and that I had heard good things about her teaching style. I then told her I was a Christian and that I find it offensive when people say G - d - -. It's like nails on a chalkboard to me. She then expressed how glad she was that I brought this to her attention. That conversation created a connection, and connections with profs are sometimes hard to come by.

My philosophy professor was sensitive to this throughout the rest of the semester. Sometimes she would slip up and then glance at me like a kid caught with a hand in the cookie jar. When professors are generous and sensitive enough to offer an open invitation like that, seize the moment and take them up on it. The professor was genuine and sincere in issuing the invitation. By taking her up on it, she was reminded that there are still those who take their belief systems seriously.

That professor was also something else — she was a contrast to other professors who mocked opposing views in the classroom. While this professor made it clear what her views were, for the most part she attempted to treat other views with a measure of respect. It's what's known as civility. While our personal views were often polarized, she became one of my favorite professors. I have great respect and admiration for her.

YOU CAN WRITE!

Helping ignite discussion is exciting. Excitement can still exist among the feelings of isolation and loneliness. There are a lot of different ways to tell the other side of a story.

Weekly, you have an opportunity to write letters to the editor. Campus newspapers vary, but our campus newspaper is filled with articles in dubious taste on a regular basis. It is not often that one will read a conservative article among its pages.

One week, the paper did a feature story on most embarrassing moments. These weren't the typical "I walked into the wrong restroom" or "I was wearing three-inch heels and fell face down getting my diploma" type stories. My friends and I sat in my dorm room reading the paper together. When we came upon this feature we erupted in simultaneous gagging and shocked screams.

The campus paper had clearly demonstrated it had no class, at least in that issue. Next to each embarrassing story was a graphic of a trophy. These anonymous contributors were being commended for their immorality. The funny thing is, if they were proud enough of their most embarrassing moments to write them up for the campus paper, why didn't they want their names printed next to their dirty deeds?

I'd never written a letter to the editor before. I thought it over and then decided to go for it. Here's what I sent:

> Shame on the paper for stooping so low as to print the repulsive anecdotes submitted in the weekend mishap hall-of-famers. I was obviously under an erroneous impression of the paper. I expected a college newspaper to print the news, sports, and occasional page-filling drivel, but where is the justification for devoting two pages to such nauseating rubbish? Just because these disreputable acts go on does not make them newsworthy. As for their entertainment value, where is the humor in reading about the depraved low lives engaging in oral sex, threesomes, and kissing as if it were a sport? By highlighting and celebrating animal-like behavior the student newspaper denigrates the reputation and academic climate of the university. I would like to offer my congratulations to the student newspaper for enhancing my postulation that many students esteem glorifying an empty lifestyle of reckless immorality over intellectualism and integrity.

I may have come on a little strong. Okay, a lot strong. I fired with both barrels and I was curious (make that worried) to see what kind of response the letter would get. The reaction from other students was a shock. They were really supportive. I hadn't anticipated that. People stopped me in the hall and walking to class. A few grabbed me in class to tell me they completely agreed. My roommate overheard students reading my letter aloud together in the dorm lobby and they were impressed with it. My resident assistant stopped by, saying I did a great job and that I was right on the money. Even a friend's parents who subscribe to the college newspaper were encouraged and passed along favorable comments.

Of course, there's no sense in letting your ego get inflated — there will always be someone else to take it back down to size for you. Near the end of the year, a student wrote an article criticizing Campus Crusade for Christ on a national level. The next week he wrote another article criticizing our own school's Campus Crusade for Christ. He took things out of context and twisted the facts to end up with a gross misrepresentation of what Campus Crusade is all about. I hated to see such slander go unchecked, so I decided to write a letter to the editor. I made the point that while the writer's piece addressed Campus Crusade, what he was really attacking was orthodox Christianity. I considered my letter direct and to the point. I obviously got my point across to a senior who wrote a letter to the editor the next week responding to my letter. He said he was "ashamed to even consider Ms. Nye a fellow [student], especially in light of [the university's President's] efforts to promote and increase diversity on campus. . . . I wish you'd transfer somewhere more ideal and get the hell out of here, rather than representing our school in such a disgraceful fashion. . . . I'm sad to say that I don't see much hope for our campus either, especially with people like Ms. Nye in our freshman class."

I wasn't the only one who had written in defense of Campus Crusade. A number of students had. While you have a standing opportunity to be heard in the student newspaper, opportunities in the classroom aren't as frequent.

I had an unusual opportunity one day in philosophy class near the end of the semester. The professor was discussing evil, all the pain in the world, and how it's hard to believe that a good God exists. The discussion was sincere and heartfelt. She wasn't baiting anybody or antagonizing anybody — she was asking a real question and engaging the class in thought. The problem of pain is a very real dilemma. It seemed as though the door had swung open wide. I was nervous, but I knew it was a perfect segue to present the fact that Jesus himself was not immune from suffering and sorrow. I said that Jesus suffered the greatest pain dying on the cross. It was a pain that He did not deserve but chose to endure for our redemption, in order that we may believe in Him and be saved. I spoke for only a minute or two, but when I finished, I realized I had presented the gospel message in a nutshell. Now, I was really nervous.

The response wasn't quite what I expected. I was surprised when the following week two people approached me and responded positively. One said, "Wow, I can't believe you said that." The other said, "Hey, I really agreed with what you had to say." Moments like that fuel the tank and keep you going. It may not always look like it, but people are listening and people are asking hard questions and looking for answers.

Never, never, never assume you're alone, even if you don't see or hear someone else speaking up. And remember, when one person speaks up, others will follow.

FEMINISM, ANYONE?

Of course, not all of my attempts to make a difference have been successful. Disastrous would be more like it.

I was at a Campus Crusade leader's retreat where we listened to a speaker saying that we should accept God's call to reach the entire campus. One way we could do that was to find out what non-Christians care about and attempt to care about those things, too. The speaker used the example of joining the feminist group on campus. He said he personally promotes himself as a First Wave Feminist, meaning he believes women should have the right to vote. He said it gets their attention when he says he's a feminist, and once they find out what he really thinks about feminism, he already has a foot in the door to begin a conversation.

After listening to this, I initially thought it was a goofy idea. I also thought it was so misleading. Personally, I didn't want to be known as a feminist. But as I considered what the speaker said about attempting to reach out to others, I felt somewhat convicted. At a Block Party, I put my name on the feminist listserve.

I haven't had a chance to attend a meeting, but I still get the minutes from each meeting by e-mail. After several months of reading their minutes, I'm hesitant to go to a meeting. The most recent minutes included the Hanger Project. Campus feminists want to place hangers around campus with statistics about how many women die from botched abortions. No mention of how many babies die from abortions, just "womyn."

I also can't see myself blending in with a crowd rooting for getting birth control, condoms, and the morning after pill distributed on campus. Ditto for supporting V-Day, groups doing the *Vagina Monologues.*

Being part of a group like this could conceivably be a vehicle for outreach, but I no longer feel compelled to join, just as I no longer feel compelled to seize each and every opportunity to make a difference. You have to be selective, you have to choose your moments carefully, and above all, you have to be sincere.

PLUGGING IN

Another way to fortify yourself is by keeping in touch with old friends from high school by e-mail, phone calls, letters, and by praying for one another. However, the absolutely, positively most important thing on the "survive and thrive" list at college is to plug into a church and/or a para-church organization. The great thing is that every campus has at least one, and many of the larger campuses have more than one, para-church organization on campus. There's Campus Crusade for Christ (CCC), Navigators, Inter-Varsity, and some lesser-known ones that are excellent, as well.

At the first Campus Crusade meeting of the year, a friend and I shared the edge of a window ledge in the very back of the large classroom as students squeezed in. All the seats were taken, including the steps. The room was packed. We began to sing worship songs.

You are the Lord of lords
You are the King of kings
You are the Mighty God
You are Lord of earth,
You are Emanuel
You are the Living God.

It was amazing to hear everyone sing with such passion. I had been told that I would be inspired by the Christians at secular colleges. I was already impressed by the enthusiasm. It was also encouraging because these students were coming to Campus Crusade because they wanted to, not because it was a mandatory chapel meeting such as those at most Christian colleges. As worship ended, someone stood up and gave a message. The message was about how to begin a relationship with God. It was good "getting-started stuff" for someone in the room who might be asking questions for the first time.

Finding a church and a para-church group to be part of is an absolute must. It doesn't work to be a Lone Ranger Christian. You'll be swept away and you will not grow spiritually unless you have the accountability and encouragement that comes from Christian relationships.

Ask any Christian student to explain the instant bond you have with fellow Christians and they may not be able to put words to it, but they understand. When Christians are the minority on a secular campus, that bond becomes even more special. I have friends with similar interests, friends in my major, friends in my extracurricular activities, but the friends that I share the bond of Christ with stand apart. Maybe it's because those relationships are more rare on a secular campus so they become more precious, or maybe it's because of the power of the acknowledgment of Christ's love.

Because I go to a smaller university, there were not as many Christian organizations to choose from. Fortunately, CCC had a strong and active presence on campus, with participation of close to

ten percent of the student body. CCC, similar to most Christian organizations, does a lot of advertising the week before classes start in
order to get people interested and involved. Campus Crusade also
does a lot of outreach geared toward freshman specifically. On the
campus I attend they have a student-led "freshman outreach team"
that plans fun activities and socials specifically for freshmen so that
they can make new friends and, at the same time, grow spiritually.
Our CCC staff leaders live right next to campus and they open up
their house at all hours to students. The back door to their basement
is unlocked so students can go there and hang out, have Bible studies, or worship. It's a very cool house and a favorite hang-out among
many of the students involved in Crusade.

In addition to plugging into a Christian organization on campus, it's important to be involved in a smaller Bible study. Commonly, groups such as CCC or InterVarsity offer small group Bible
studies led by staff or upperclassmen. Bible studies provide opportunities to get to know people on a deeper level, keep each other accountable, and really dig into the Word. Christian organizations on
campus have a tough job. They try to meet the needs of established
Christians, yet at the same time keep an eye out for new Christians
and those who may still be sitting on the fence. As a result, sometimes the small group Bible studies may not go very far beneath
the surface. You really can't generalize because there are so many
variables, including the group leader and the make-up and maturity
of the group members. Keeping things simple in small groups, in
an attempt to make people at all stages of growth feel welcome and
to encourage students to bring their non-Christian friends, has its
ups and downs. You may get tired of hearing the salvation message preached every week, but for some students it may be the first
time they've ever heard that message. Exercise your options when it
comes to plugging into a small group study.

I asked one of the moms I had babysat for if she would lead a
Bible study for a group of my friends. We liked the opportunity to
get off campus and go to a real home, eat good food, and learn from

a seasoned Christian woman. The Bible study was also flexible to accommodate our busy schedules and we were able to choose what we wanted to study.

A close friend of mine at a huge university took the initiative to start her own Bible study with her close friends. It was actually called a GIG — Groups Investigating God. It was a six-week Bible study to introduce people interested in Christianity to the basic beliefs of Christianity.

Connecting with Christians on campus will pose a unique experience for students, depending on their interests, worship style, and spiritual needs. There is no magic formula or one way to do things. I gathered e-mails from a few of my friends at secular schools to learn more about how they connected with other Christians. While they all had different experiences, there is one common thread — they all stress the importance of connecting with Christians right away.

If you're scouting out a school and wonder what type of para-church groups are on campus, it might be helpful to visit the websites and see who has a chapter on campus. At the back of this book, under Resources, you'll find brief profiles of the major campus ministries and their website addresses.

HINDSIGHT

First things first

Find a para-church group on campus, a church, a small Bible study, one of the above, or all three. Make it one of the first things you do. You're setting your foundation.

Chalking

When you pack to go to college, in addition to taking a tap light, shower caddy, and twin x-long sheets, take an ample supply of chalk for chalking. On most campuses, chalking is like legal graffiti, a new way to practice freedom of speech. You can write your opinions or thought-provoking questions on the sidewalk one day and the rain washes them away the next.

Outta here

Sometimes you vacillate between reaching out and protecting yourself. Many times, in the interest of surviving and thriving, it is necessary to get completely away from campus. College is not the "real world," and it is important to be reminded of that. Break away now and then. Go for a bike ride, go roller-blading, go for a walk, but get off campus and remind yourself that there is life outside of the bubble.

Scripture memory

Scripture memory has been a great help in thriving on campus. Having gone to a Christian high school, we were required to memorize multiple verses every week. I really didn't think much of it at the time. The majority of the time I hurriedly memorized the verses in the class prior to Bible class. But they stuck with me. I experienced God using that in ways I never had before. Whenever I was facing a struggle, whether it was loneliness, doubt, hurt, or anger, relevant verses would pop into my head. Inside, I would be saying, *I can't stand this place, I'm so alone.* Then a verse would spring to mind, "I will never leave you nor forsake you" (Josh. 1:5). I'd be thinking, *I can't stand this place, I'm so hurt and worn down.* Then I'd remember the Scripture, "Blessed are those who are persecuted because of righteousness, for theirs is the kingdom of heaven" (Matt. 5:10).

You've Got Mail

From: "Katie and Natalie"

To: "Abby"

Subject: Friends

Natalie and I are sitting in the library and decided to answer your questions about making Christian connections on campus together. In philosophy, our professor challenged us to be willing to let go of (suspend) our beliefs, preconceptions, and enter philosophy in the pursuit of truth. He stated we were only allowed to think on the "human side of things." He stated: "Why should anyone care what a young, uneducated, inexperienced, naive person would think?" If we tried to use the Bible in our papers, he would say that it was irrelevant and didn't count toward our argument.

Having this type of experience is both challenging to one's faith, but also can be beneficial if the Christian becomes stronger because of it. Natalie and I were able to "get through" this class because we knew each other as Christians and were comforted by the thought that it is not ridiculous to think that God does exist. We need to think for ourselves and hold onto truth and not cast it aside for a class, simply because we have already searched and have found the truth, namely that God does exist and that Jesus Christ is our Savior. We found encouragement from the verse Colossians 2:8, and from other Christian groups and friends that we met via Campus Crusade for Christ and church. Fellowship from Christian friends can greatly impact your own relationship with God. One last piece of advice is to think for yourself, and see how professors teachings compare to the Bible and the truth found there.

Natalie and Katie

Fish Out of Water

From: "Chris"

To: "Abby"

Subject: Co-op

For me, the most important way of plugging into a Christian community was through where I lived. This could apply not only to a cooperative house such as the one I live in, but also to any other living situation. If you are going to live in an apartment or a dorm, I would suggest finding another Christian or two to do so with, even if he isn't your best friend. The people that you live with are the ones that you will be seeing on a consistent basis, who will know how you are doing with this area or that, and will be able to keep you accountable, more so than someone who you see less often.

Fairway, which is a house of 50-some Christian guys, provides the Christian fellowship and camaraderie that is always around me. Because of this, I always have somebody to turn to with problems as little as homework to bigger things such as deaths.

If Ryan doesn't email you, I know he has done something similar. He lived with Dave for the first year, and after that moved in with a group of Christian guys he met through Navigators.

Chris

From: "Mark"

To: "Abby"

Subject: Connecting

When I arrived on campus in the fall, I knew absolutely no one; none of my family members had ever attended here and no one from my school had even applied here before. Since then, I have made friends that will last a lifetime and are built upon a mutual love of Christ. This campus has a reputation of being a party school, which I soon discovered was well-earned after just one week. I wanted to distance myself from the alcohol aspect of college, and searched out Christian organizations before classes even began. Fortunately for me, different groups such as Campus Crusade for Christ, Navigators, and Intervarsity Christian Fellowship all advertised heavily during the week before the start of class. Despite their efforts to attract students, the voices of the Christian groups were out-shouted by messages for liberal student groups, such as GLBT. I noticed during my first week that liberal organizations received public support and outright endorsement from the university.

Of all the Christian groups I visited, I felt God's presence the most in Campus Crusade's ministry. I had heard of the organization before. Upon walking in the door of the building for the first meeting of the year, I was approached quickly by an enthusiastic man by the name of Joel. It turned out that Joel was in charge of all the Campus Crusade Bible studies in the area of campus that I lived, and so he immediately invited me to a weekly study. After several weeks, attending the study became habit, and the seven or eight young men that made up the small group have become good friends of mine. For me, joining a small group at the beginning of the year was a crucial step in my ever-growing relationship with Christ. God was able to use our small group to give each of us somewhere to find accountability and strength. Finding a group of Christians would have been much harder and nearly impossible without the organizing capability of a functioning ministry, such as Campus Crusade.

Over the course of my freshman year, I did meet other Christians in different settings, such as class, and a few that lived on my floor, but I have not grown as close to them as I have to the ones in my study. Another important aspect of my Bible study that enabled me to grow greatly in the Lord was the fact that it was all male. I found it much easier to learn and grow in God's Word while around other men who also had a hunger and desire to know God to a fuller extent. Another aspect of Campus Crusade that helped college students in their walk with faith is its weekly meetings entitled "College Life," where roughly four hundred Christians come together in the biggest lecture hall on campus. The sheer size of the gathering shows Christians who feel alone on the huge liberal campus that there are other brothers and sisters out there who want to help spread God's Word.

God also made sure that I would find strong Christians in random places. One such example is my RA. I discovered that he was also a brother in Christ after one week, and we instantly felt the connection that brings believers together. Upon entering college, I did not expect that my RA would become one of my close friends, much less the fact that we would discuss God's love and how to live in the Spirit. In addition to having an RA that was a great brother in Christ, I often saw people from my classes showing up at Crusade events. Once again, as soon as I talked to any of them, the strong bond of Christ between believers was formed.

The most helpful Christian connections I made during my freshman year occurred over spring break. I traveled down to Panama City Beach with about 20 other Christians from Campus Crusade for a convention labeled the Big Break. The purpose of the convention was to reach out to the lost students on the beach and evangelization training that could be taken back and applied on campus. The most important aspect that I took away from the trip was the formation of 20 new great friends. I knew none of my fellow spring breakers when I left on a Friday afternoon for the beach, but by the week's end we were practically family. It was through a trip that God made our friendships possible, and one put on by a well-organized ministry.

I am a firm believer in the concept that God uses organized campus ministries to reach a large number of lost students on university campuses across the nation. Students that become involved, such as those in my Bible study, grow much more over the course of their time in college than those who find no group of believers to fellowship with. It is hard to grow in the Spirit without the support of other Christians. God's love shows itself daily through the lives of the Christian connections I see around campus.

Mark

You've Got Mail

From: "Vanessa T"

To: "Abby"

Dear Abby,

I think going from a Christian high school to a secular college or university is a big transition no matter how strong a believer you are. This is the situation I faced upon graduating from high school. I didn't become involved in Christian groups on campus but I did make a conscious effort to stay connected with other strong Christian friends. E-mail is great for keeping each other updated, encouraged, accountable, and laughing. Having a strong core of people gives me the stability to grow and reach out to others (Christians or non-Christians).

Most students graduating from a Christian high school have a mentor type person they can talk with — hang on to that relationship. Advice and opinions are never difficult to find on a college campus but GOOD advice can be scarce. Having a growing, godly mentor who speaks the truth is invaluable.

College work requires a lot of dedication. It is easy to get caught up in work and social activities and let your relationship with the Lord fade. Tools I have found useful are prioritizing and budgeting time. Make a list (literally) of important things, then make a list of the time each requires. While doing this, I realized I did not have enough time for all my interests. Simplify. If your aspirations do not allow you time to spend cultivating a relationship with the Lord, adjust your aspirations. Having a hard copy of your priorities will make adjustments easier and clear . . . well, maybe not always easier.

Abby, that is what is off the top of my head right now. Ahh, gotta go to class. Right now.

From: "VanCan"

To: "Abby"

Subject: Connecting

Hi, Abby,

Could you have asked a harder question? :) Before where I wanted to attend college, I made sure to find out if there were any active Christian groups on campus. When I first decided to go to Pitt, some friends from home, who work with InterVarsity Christian Fellowship (IV), gave me contact information for an IV chapter at Pitt.

After arriving at Pitt I quickly got in touch with IV. Unfortunately, they didn't have a group going at Pitt at that present moment in time so I attended their chapter meetings at a university right down the road. I really enjoyed it, but had been hoping to get involved with a Christian group on my campus. After a few weeks at Pitt I quickly learned about several different Christian groups. It was a little overwhelming trying to figure out how to pick a group to get involved with and find a church to attend.

One group I visited held weekly meetings where a little over 100 students gathered for a time of worship and teaching. This group, Cornerstone, was headed by the Coalition for Christian Outreach (CCO). I found out about this group because they met at a church directly across the street from my dorm. Initially, I struggled with the group's large size and what I thought were less challenging teachings than I was used to. However, once I began to get involved in a small group Bible study with girls from Cornerstone, I got more plugged in and was more challenged in my own personal growth. I learned that the purpose of a Christian community is not all about me and what I can get out of it. That is definitely an added bonus and I think what should eventually result from being involved in a Christian community. However, the focus should be on other Christians and our mutual support, encouragement, and desire to share Christ with others who don't know about what He has done for them. It has taken me a while to see that I have been very selfish about trying to find a Christian group on campus. Now that I realize I should be trying to serve others, I have been even more blessed.

From my experience, I would say you have to be fairly pro-active in your search for a Christian group and other Christians. You can't sit around and expect a Christian to approach you and invite you to their church or group. That's great if it does happen, but from my experiences that doesn't happen too often. Don't get me wrong. I think personal invitation is the most effective way to get someone to attend an event or meeting, but it can be unproductive just waiting around for someone to do so for you. You have to put yourself in places where you can meet other Christians. The biggest hindrance for me in finding a Christian community at Pitt was getting over the fact that there is no perfect group. Each ministry may have a slightly different focus, different style of worship, different format for meetings, and be composed of all kinds of different people. I had to let go of my perfect preconceived ideas and just jump into a group that I knew was seeking to teach the truth about God and glorify Him in all they did. Once you find a group or groups that are teaching and living out biblical truths, it really doesn't matter where you get plugged in. As I've done so, I've met more Christians and begun to feel more "spiritually stable" at school.

Also, occasionally attending other Christian group meetings and functions has helped me to recognize more Christians on campus and to feel more united with them.

Other groups on campus are Campus Crusade for Christ, Cross-seekers, Chi-Alpha, Ambassadors for Christ, and Christian Student Fellowship.

I hope this helps.

Love,

V

Fish Out of Water

From: "Ben"

To: "Abby"

Subject: Hanging out

As far as connecting with other Christians go, well I think it depends on how much you want to connect with them . . . are you fired up about Christ and long to talk to others about Him whether it be with other believers or not or are you an apathetic Christian who is either scared to show your real identity or find more pleasure in not bringing up the topic of God because you don't want to give your all to Christ in the way you live. Many Christians say they believe yet still love things of the world and hence find shame in revealing their identity in Christ. So are we ashamed to be a Christian? . . . Mark 8:38 says, "If anyone is ashamed of me and my words in this adulterous and sinful generation, the Son of Man will be ashamed of him when he comes in his Father's glory with the holy angels." So are we out to please man or God. Where is our fear placed?

I think if you really have a desire to connect with other Christians you will find them. So it is more of a matter of desire.

Benjamin

You've Got Mail

From: "Rachel"

To: "Abby"

Subject: Greek IV

Abby,

I never really got involved with Campus Crusade, which is pretty big here, but I did immediately connect with Greek InterVarsity. Greek InterVarsity is a program for, but not necessarily limited to, guys and girls in sororities and fraternities. I got involved with Greek IV before I was even in my sorority (AXiD) because the man who started it not only locally, but nationally, Andy Dalton, is financially sponsored by my dad. Dad told me it would be a good thing for me to check out so Kelsey and I went a couple of times and loved it, and sure enough, I'm still going every Thursday night. The great thing about Greek IV is how receptive the people there are. As soon as you walk in the door, you're hugged, welcomed, etc. Even if you're not a familiar face, people will walk up to you immediately and introduce themselves and make you feel welcome. The thing that is bad for outsiders is that it is a program for students in the Greek system. Even though, as mentioned before, it's not limited to us, people outside of the Greek system don't really attend so they never get to see how much fun the whole thing is. It's one of the best programs I've ever gotten involved in. Actually, there might be one thing. My friend, Laura, who is a senior in our house, started going just this year b/c she hadn't even heard of the program before, which she wished she would have b/c she loves it so much. So I guess the worst thing about it is you have to dig for programs to get involved in.

Rachel

Christian
thinking is a rare
and difficult thing; so
many seem unaware that
the first great commandment
according to our Lord is,
"Thou shalt love the
Lord thy God . . .
with all thy
mind."

— Oswald Chambers

Epilogue

In the middle of the second semester, Campus Crusade for Christ distributed free copies of *Mind Siege*, a book by Tim La-Haye and David Noebel. It was a great read while on campus. *Mind Siege* cataloged a few campus stories that had a familiar ring.

An anguished mother told LaHaye and Noebel of her daughter who was raised in Christian schools and in a Christian home and was taught Christian values and morals. The girl enrolled at the University of Oregon, a school the mother calls "one of the most liberal universities in the nation." The girl was overwhelmed by her professors and began to believe their philosophies. She has turned her back on God.

The authors also tell the story of a student at Southern Oregon University who enrolled in calculus, physics, chemistry, and organ classes. The girl made the honor roll first quarter with grades of A in calculus, physics, and organ, and a B in chemistry. The University is not permitting the girl to return next year. Why? "She has refused to take the university's three-quarter, four-unit-per-quarter, total-immersion indoctrination course in the Oregon State Religion," a religion the father describes as the university's own brand of "atheistic secular humanism."

The father says, "The course text opens with a 13-page article on rape, including detailed descriptions of actual rapes — which sets the stage for teaching feminism — and goes downhill from there."

Why is it so tough to get a college education without all the baggage, without all the indoctrination?

I struggled to put many things in perspective my freshman year. Yes, I expected different opinions at college. I expected different viewpoints on topics and I expected professors would passionately share their opinions. But I thought the personal opinions and viewpoints would be relevant to the coursework and that the topics would flow from a syllabus, not an agenda.

I was restless on campus. They say to give yourself two to four weeks to settle in and adjust. I had adjusted. I had adjusted to cafeteria food, dorm life, and a communal bathroom. But I was still uneasy. Maybe I had a slow adjustment curve and needed a little more time. Maybe this place would fit like a good pair of jeans by mid-terms. Or Thanksgiving. Or maybe by December. I sure hoped I'd settled in before finals week began. Some days it didn't look too promising.

It was hard to put into words exactly what it was that kept me on edge. I think it could best be described as a campus ethos that was unsettling. There was a mentality and culture that in some ways actually discouraged critical thought. Ideas weren't dissected as much as swallowed whole without analysis or thought. That surprised me. It caught me off guard.

Besides the ethos, I'm sure I suffered from a naiveté that expected a level playing field. There was a wave of disillusionment that accompanied that hard reality.

It was difficult not to project that disappointment and that disillusionment toward the whole campus or the entire college experience. I thought I had a handle on that "in the world, not of the world" business, but maybe I didn't. Maybe I wasn't cut out to mix it up. Maybe I was destined to give up my Very Cherry nail polish, strappy sandals, blonde highlights, and join the Amish.

Because of the odd and aggressive mix of teachers I'd drawn, teachers often on the prowl for conservatives and Christians to re-program and re-educate, there were times I felt absolutely defeated. I knew it wasn't true, but I remember one day in particular when I felt outnumbered and completely alone. I prayed God would give me perspective. I was walking to class feeling bummed and I passed an upperclassman who I knew was a bold Christian. He and I were going to talk about my classes the next day.

A half-block later, I passed my faculty-in-residence member, who is a Christian. We had been going to the same church. She said hello, I said hello. It wasn't much, but it was encouragement. God had directed my steps in advance so that I would run into those specific people and be reminded that I was not alone. It was good to be reminded I wasn't alone, but was that enough?

I could find a good Christian school to go to, so why go through this? I was more than ready to throw in the towel. Maybe I'd take a white T-shirt and wave it from a stick.

A friend had come into town and we attended a party for a congressional candidate after the polls had closed on election day. After the party, we were walking downtown and he asked if my dif-ficulties adjusting to college stemmed from being so sheltered at a Christian high school, from being thrown out into the world and being shocked at what was going on. He suggested it would just take time and that I would get used to it.

Did I really want to get used to that? Why would I want to get used to the lack of shame and civility around me? I didn't want to grow numb and begin thinking that unhealthy was healthy. Getting used to it would mean developing a callousness and desensitization. If we're desensitized to the degradation around us, we won't be able to identify it, let alone stand apart from it or help change it. It may sound like I was mad, and at times I'm sure I was. I wasn't as angry at what I saw as I was sad.

There were many days I silently envied my friends on Christian campuses. They were connecting with a wide circle of new people, having fun, and listening to engaging speakers and taking stimulating classes.

Meanwhile, here I was on this secular campus listening to Christianity mocked and ridiculed in the classroom. More and more I found myself agreeing with John Nash, the main character in *A Beautiful Mind* who never went to class because "class will dull the mind."

When friends asked how I liked school during my freshman year I could hardly bring myself to feign a benign answer. I loathed school. But I didn't say that, I'd say it was fine and change the subject.

A friend of the family asked me how college was going. I told her about all the indoctrination and politically correct nonsense happening in the classroom. She nodded sympathetically and said, "My son had that problem when he went to college, but then he figured out how to play the game. You just have to learn to give them what they want."

Give them what they want? When pigs fly.

There were times I thought maybe I wasn't cut out for a secular school. Maybe I had made a terrible mistake. But I'd done my homework. I'd visited a half-dozen colleges and ranked them with a point system on criteria such as location, size, majors available, scholarship monies, academic environment, and H.Q. (hottie quotient, how cute the guys were). I narrowed my options down to two schools. It was between this secular private school with the program of study I could finish in four years, a program that often takes five or six at other schools, and a high-profile Christian college known as the ivy-league of the evangelicals.

The private secular school, like so many others, prided itself on high entrance requirements, diversity, and attention to the individual student. The school came with a very hefty price tag, but it also came with generous scholarship money. As far as ideology, the school was considered by most to be moderate.

I went back and forth on the Christian school versus non-Christian school arguments. A lot of my Christian friends fell in line with the thinking of James Dobson. Dobson points out that many of today's universities, once the moral and intellectual trendsetters for society, have now included relativism and excluded God. Dobson says, "For this reason, it's essential that Christian parents and students consider a university's spiritual climate as well as its academic offerings. While it's possible for young people to hold on to — and even share — their faith on a secular campus, they should be aware of the diverse and erroneous viewpoints they're likely to encounter in their classes and social interaction. Since the college years are a pivotal time for personal growth, students may find that a Christian college helps them establish a world view rooted in their faith and provides training that will assist them in understanding and defending their beliefs."

Dobson makes a valid point — a point I was learning firsthand. But there is also the viewpoint that when you attend a Christian college you are insulating yourself from the real world. The critics contend that far from being salt and light, you become part of a holy huddle. It was an argument I wrestled with many times. Sometimes I argued in favor of the Christian college and other times I convinced myself the place for me was a secular school. To this day I can argue either side of the argument with equal degrees of passion.

Then there's the matter of practicality. Private colleges are more expensive. Also, many small Christian schools do not offer degrees or programs of study that the larger universities do.

After much thought, I had decided to follow the program of study at the secular school and looked forward to mixing it up on a secular campus. I didn't have any idea how tough "mixing it up" could be. At times, I was not only disgusted by the environment, I was disgusted by myself.

I found myself tempted to get down on their level. I wanted to practice tolerance the way they practiced tolerance — only tolerate people who thought like me, and shred everybody else. I wanted to return some of the pain they'd delivered to me. I knew I couldn't respond this way.

Struggling with my reaction to circumstances around me, I shared my thoughts in an e-mail with one of my friends at a Christian school. I asked him what he would say to a professor who was blatantly anti-Christian. My friend responded: "I'd simply tell him, 'Say hello to Lucifer on your way down to the barbeque.' " Funny, but not a big help. While he was joking, it made me wish he were here, and a few of my other friends as well, because they are excellent debaters. They're smart, assertive, and can be aggressive when need be. They have the intellectual and debate skills it takes to survive on a secular campus — but they chose to go to Christian colleges.

Clearly, I could not tell my professor to say hello to Lucifer on the way down to the barbeque. I knew what I had to do. Be polite and kind. Maintain a loving spirit. Keep my voice calm. Not lose my temper. Use the soft answer that turns away wrath. Love my enemies. Pray for those who persecute me.

First semester freshman year was the worst. Some significant changes came with the second semester. I had a humanities professor that restored some of my faith in education. She taught the classics and her class was tough. It was demanding, challenging, and thought-provoking. We read Kierkegaard's *Fear and Trembling*, which revolves around the Old Testament story of Abraham's answering God's call to sacrifice his son Isaac. Surprisingly, we didn't spend class arguing the existence of God, or the validity of the Bible, but took Kierkegaard's literature for what it was. We examined it and analyzed it without beating faith to a bloody pulp. Instead, the conclusion was one of high regard for faith.

The class offered a heavy reading schedule of worthy books and a steep learning curve. Maybe that experience wouldn't be the last. Maybe there were more pockets of academic integrity.

As I mentioned before, I also had a philosophy professor who was staunchly liberal, but who was also civil. That class, too, was a welcome breath of fresh air. The science classes continued on track, conducted in a professional manner and sticking to subject matters of chemistry and biology. The classes have been tough, challenging, and invigorating and the profs outstanding.

In addition, I kept reflecting on a dose of encouragement that came from a faculty member and mentor in the health sciences just days before the Christmas break. He and I had exchanged some e-mails in which I expressed my frustration with the struggles I faced being a conservative and Christian on a secular campus. I didn't know if he was a Christian, but I knew he lives in the real world, is in touch with reality, and conducts himself like a professional. I know he is fair and honest and respects genuine diversity of opinion. We were going over my schedule for second semester and, knowing my frustrations, he encouraged me to stay. He encouraged me to look at my education in terms of more than getting a degree, but in terms of being a student who could make a difference.

Now that more time has passed since I began taking notes that would become the first chapter of this book, I'm at the end of my third year and have gained more perspective. My hope is that this book would do that for you — help you know what to expect. It made a big difference knowing what was ahead.

I was invited to be part of the freshman outreach team with Campus Crusade the summer preceding my sophomore year. Our team had a lot of work to do before classes even started. We were involved with the freshman right from the get-go, literally waiting at the curb to help them move in the first day. We manned survey tables and tried to strike up conversations with the freshmen. For those who marked on their survey that they were interested in Christianity, Campus Crusade, or Bible studies, we arranged for them to be contacted personally. One of the most successful events we planned was a freshman overnight. We went on a scavenger hunt, then two sophomores shared their testimonies, and we split into discussion groups. Afterward, there were games late into the night and worship time. Everyone had a fun time and freshmen were able to make connections with other freshman.

Having known how hard it is to be a freshman, I really had a burden to reach out to the new class of freshmen. Over the summer I put together little welcoming bags, not even knowing whom I would give them to. The bags included things to make their stay easier, such as an anti-stress mask, chalk for chalk-talk, a free ice cream coupon, Post-its, and pens. Because I was involved with the freshmen, I had unique opportunities to help them connect with each other. I was able to connect a girl that was having problems with her Wiccan roommate with another Christian girl in need of a roommate switch. They pulled off the switch and are much happier now.

In addition to reaching out to freshman, I was involved with bringing a new organization to the campus. I am vice president of Veritas. *Veritas* is Latin for truth. We want to present truth, biblical truth, in a way that will get Christians and non-Christians alike to think about the deep issues of life. We bring in a speaker once a month to address topics such as postmodernism, the authenticity of the Bible, world view, Islam, homosexuality, and evolution.

The founding process of this group started the summer after my freshman year when a few people thought the campus needed to do more to meet the needs of mature Christians and simultaneously reach out to non-Christians. What better way than to teach topics from a lecture format and then openly allow people to disagree, ask questions, and debate.

We had to get this organization approved by the Student Government Association at the beginning of the year. I was responsible for making a three-minute presentation along with the president of Veritas, answering some questions, and then leaving the room while they voted. One of the founding members of Veritas is also a part of the Student Government Association, so he stayed in the room to defend Veritas if the need arose. He told me that the first person to speak up objected to making Veritas an official organization. He was worried and thought he was going to have to jump in right away, but he didn't have to. Person after person spoke in favor of allowing us to be official. The vote passed almost unanimously. After all, we will be bringing diversity of thought to campus, and aren't we all in favor of diversity?

Although my second year saw improvements over the first year, some things didn't change. Christianity was still not tolerated in many classrooms. The English professor I had was still going after Christians. In my Islam class (a required core course), the professor insists that Jesus Christ did not think He was God. In a class titled "The Bible," students were required to read a book that went on and on about the Bible not being true or reliable. Many Christian students take that class, excited at the prospect of taking a class about Christianity. But instead of the class strengthening their faith, many have been left with unanswered questions and lingering doubts.

Some people told me that the second year would go better because I would "learn to play by their rules." Sure, that's one way to make it easier, but not if you want to sleep at night with a clean conscience. For me, second year was easier because I wasn't in as many antagonistic classes; I was in more science classes where we stick to B cells and T cells. My third year has been all medical classes, so it's gone even better. There's not as much wiggle room for indoctrination and subjectivity in the hard sciences as there is in the soft sciences.

Even though I'm not in the faith-challenging courses right now, many of my friends are. They are still speaking up. I know the thoughts that cross their minds, wondering if it's the right time to say something, the right thing to say, whether speaking up will cost them a grade, or cause them to be labeled. Most of us have those fears. But the difference between those who make a difference and those who sit silently on the sidelines is not whether you feel the fear but what you do with the fear.

May God guide you in your college decision. Wherever you go, stay the course, and run with endurance the race set before you.

ENDNOTES

Chapter 1

1. "What to Expect at College," *Focus on the Family* magazine (copyright 2000).

2. "BMOC: Big Mandate on Campus College 'Diversity' Activists Grab Freshmen at Orientation and Won't Let Go Until Everyone Holds the Same View," *WORLD* (September 14, 2002).

3. Alan Charles Kors and Harvey Silvergate, *The Shadow University* (New York, NY: Simon and Schuster, 1998).

4. "BMOC: Big Mandate on Campus College 'Diversity' Activists Grab Freshmen at Orientation and Won't Let Go Until Everyone Holds the Same View," *WORLD* (September 14, 2002).

Chapter 2

1. "Texas Two-step," *WORLD* (May 10, 2003).

2. Dinesh D'Souza, *Letters to a Young Conservative* (New York, NY: Basic Books, 2002), p. 140.

3. Ibid., p. 38.

4. Ibid., p. 40.

5. Charles Colson, "Say It Ain't So, Dave," www.breakpoint.org, January 16, 2004.

Chapter 3

1. Walter Williams, "America's Academic Tyrants," www.townhall.com, September 3, 2003.

2. Wes Vernon, *"Left-wing Campus Thought Police Harass Dissenters,"* www.newsmax.com, Nov. 27, 2002.

3. Ibid.

4. "UC-Davis Newspaper Fires Sole Conservative Columnist," *Accuracy in Academia* (January 1, 2003).

5. James Hitchcock, "Cardinal Arinze's Pro-life, Pro-family Comments Anger Georgetown Faculty Members, Spark Protest," *Women for Faith and Family* (May 23, 2003).

6. Ibid.

7. "Blind Guides, Cultural Malaise, and the VMI Dinner Prayer," *The Rutherford Institute* (August 18, 2003).

8. Ibid.

9. Charles Colson, "Hitting the Wall," www.breakpoint.org, September 2, 2003.

10. Nicholas Taborek, "Democrats Riled by Race-, Gender-biased Bake Sale," *Daily Bruin*, February 17, 2003.

11. George Archibad, "Miss America Silenced," *Washington Times*, October 9, 2002.

Chapter 4

1. Ron Howell, "Defeat Troops, Professor Says; Wants a Million Mogadishus," *Newsday* (March 28, 2003).

2. "Girls, Pearls, and Indoctrination Machines," *Independent Women's Forum* (January 2000).

3. Ibid.

4. Matt Kaufman, "Power PC," www.boundless.org, Focus on the Family, 1998.

5. Laura Schlessinger, "America Is Afraid," www.worldnetdaily.com, November 11, 2002.

Chapter 5

1. Josh McDowell, *The New Tolerance* (Wheaton, IL: Tyndale House Publishers, Inc., 1998), p. 9.

2. Ibid.

3. Elisabeth Elliott, *A Lamp Unto My Feet* (Ventura, CA: Gospel Light Publications, 2004).

Chapter 6

1. David Horowitz, "The Problem with America's Colleges," www.Townhall.com, September 5, 2002.

2. "Christian Coach Denied Job Because of Faith, Views on Homosexuals," *Culture Facts* (April 18, 2002).

3. "Intolerant Tolerance: Anti-Christian Bigotry on Campus," The Christian Broadcast Network, July 10, 2002.

4. "Indiana U Attacks a Conservative Prof," *Chronicle of Higher Education* (November 5, 2003).

Chapter 7

1. "Effects of Heavy Drinking in College on Study Effort, Grade Point Average, and Major Choice," *Bell and Howell Information and Learning* (October 2002).

2. Elliott N. Neal, "Binge Drinking Doubled at Women's Colleges," *Harvard Crimson* (April 1, 2002).

3. "Effects of Heavy Drinking in College on Study Effort, Grade Point Average, and Major Choice," *Bell and Howell Information and Learning* (October 2002).

4. Joe Haley, "Walk of Shame," *Butler Collegian*, November 6, 2002.

5. Wendy Shalit, *A Return to Modesty: Discovering a Lost Virtue* (New York, NY: Free Press, 1999), p. 193.

6. "Daughters of the Sexual Revolution," *Independent Women's Forum* (Autumn 2000).

7. Joshua Harris, *I Kissed Dating Goodbye* (Sisters, OR: Multnomah Publishers, 2003), p. 93.

Chapter 9

1. "Recovering the Art of Christian Polemics," *New Oxford Review* (October 2002).

Resources

As I've read and done research on the college experience for this book, I've come across a lot of material and websites that are helpful. They are items of interest to any college student interested in engaging culture, be it on a secular campus or a Christian campus. I pass them along, with the hope that they may be encouraging to you.

You may be familiar with these sites; if not, it's worth your time to check them out. Many of them are useful for obtaining a biblical perspective and background on issues. Others are helpful for doing research for papers. There are news sites, faith-based sites, a few political sites, some Bible study sites with tons of helpful study aids (one of them lets you subscribe to daily devotionals that are delivered to your in-box), and one site that is just plain fun.

WEBSITES

www.agapepress.com

Sponsored by American Family Association, this is an online summary of daily news. Regularly features news items of particular interest to Christians and carries a breadth of commentary.

www.answersingenesis.org

Answers in Genesis is the largest creationist ministry in the world. Their website is filled with helpful articles for defending your faith. Many college professors try to attack biblical creation, but the resources on AiG's website will provide solid scientific evidence for the reality of the Bible's account.

www.backtothebible.org

Back to the Bible describes themselves as "a worldwide Christian ministry dedicated to leading people into a dynamic relationship with God. Using radio, TV, the Internet, and other media, we share the Gospel message and help Christians grow to spiritual maturity. With broadcasts in more than 25 languages and an Internet reach to millions, Back to the Bible teaches the Word and touches the world."

This site is useful to mature Christians as well as new Christians. The site offers a variety of Bible study aids and devotionals, from both classical and contemporary Christian writers, delivered by e-mail daily.

www.biblegateway.com

Great site that allows you to search the Bible by key words or Scripture reference in 18 different translations of the Bible, including New American Standard, The Message, Amplified, New Living, King James, New Life, English Standard, Contemporary English, New King James, Darby Translation, and Wycliffe New Testament. Also links to a variety of helpful study resources and references.

www.boundless.org

Boundless is a very up-to-date site full of commentary and analysis on current books, movies, and issues. Hits on current issues like modesty, tattooing, short-term missions trips. If it's something you've been talking about or thinking about, Boundless is in on the discussion. Editor Blake Roeber describes the mission of the site: "As individuals and members (of families, communities, nations, cultures, and the Body of Christ), there are gaps in our lives, between what we do and *should* do, what we think and *should* think, how we feel and *should* feel. Welcome, therefore, to *Boundless*. The expression of a community defined by holy discontent, in love with Jesus Christ and (thus) painfully aware of these gaps, *Boundless* exists for the transformation of Christians through the transformation of their deepest beliefs."

www.breakpoint.org

BreakPoint is a program of the Wilberforce Forum, a division of Prison Fellowship Ministries. The site states: "Our mission is to develop and communicate Christian world view messages that offer a critique of contemporary culture and encourage and equip the church to think and live Christianly. BreakPoint provides a Christian perspective on today's news and trends via radio, interactive media, and print. Chuck Col-son's daily BreakPoint commentary airs each weekday on over 1,000 outlets with an estimated listening audience of one million people. The BreakPoint website and *Break-Point WorldView Magazine* feature Colson's commentaries as well as feature articles by other established and up-and-coming writers to equip readers with a biblical perspective on a variety of issues and topics.

www.clashradio.com

This site is hosted by Doug Giles, whom the site describes as "a proactive radio personality, speaker, and cultural analyst. His no-nonsense style of communication is a breath of fresh air in a day of stale secular and religious diatribe. Doug is senior minister of His People Miami in south Florida. Thought-provoking, edgy, with-an-attitude but still loving, commentary." In addition to links to the usual commentators, this site also links to Os Guiness, David Barton, R.C. Sproul, and Knox Theological Seminary.

www.cwfa.org

The Concerned Women for America site describes itself as "the nation's largest public policy women's organization with a rich 25-year history of helping our members across the country bring biblical principles into all levels of public policy." A great site for policy and legislative background and research. Strong biblical world view focus.

www.firstthings.com

First Things is the on-line version of the journal published by the Institute on Religion and Public Life, an inter-religious, nonpartisan research and education institute whose purpose is to advance a religiously informed public philosophy for the ordering of society. Editor-in-chief is Richard John Neuhaus.

www.frc.org

Website of the Family Research Council "Defending Faith, Family, and Freedom." This site archives policy papers on a variety of issues relevant to the Christian and culture. Excellent for research and personal backgrounding from a Christian perspective on issues in the news.

www.frontpagemag.com

Front Page Magazine is the creation of David Horowitz, recovering '60s leftist radical who is now a nationally known author and civil rights activist. Horowitz has his pulse on the college scene. He is described as "an outspoken opponent of censorship and racial preferences, and a defender of the rights of minorities and other groups under attack — including the rights of blacks, gays, women, Jews, Muslims, Christians, and white males." Excellent resources for college students. Site does a good job of mapping current trends on college campuses.

www.heritage.org

Site of the Heritage Foundation. Mission statement: Founded in 1973, the Heritage Foundation is a research and educational institute — a think tank — whose mission is to formulate and promote conservative public policies based on the principles of free enterprise, limited government, individual freedom, traditional American values, and a strong national defense. Helpful site for research papers, also carries text of speeches by movers and shakers. In-depth and thought-provoking.

www.iwf.org

Hosted by the Independent Women's Forum. Not a female-only site by any stretch, but of particular interest to females on some counts. IWF describes itself as a forum "dedicated to advancing the spirit of enterprise and self-reliance among women, and supporting the principles of political freedom, economic liberty, and personal responsibility."

IWF provides a voice for responsible, mainstream women who embrace common sense over divisive ideology. We make that voice heard in the U.S. Supreme Court, among other decision-makers in Washington, and across America's airwaves as we:

- Counter the dangerous influence of radical feminism in the courts
- Combat corrosive feminist ideology on campus
- Change the terms of the debate on quality of life issues affecting American women

Often has excellent commentary on women and the college scene.

www.Jewishworldreview.com

A news website hosted by Orthodox Jew Binyamin Jolkovsky. Mr. Jolkovsky is very friendly to conservative Christians and often posts their columns. This site is an excellent one for staying abreast of current events and gaining an orthodox Jewish perspective on news and world events.

www.lovecalculator.com

Okay, this has absolutely nothing to do with all this intellectual stuff, but if you're really, really tired of studying, it's fun to go to the love calculator and enter a few names. Back to work.

www.noindoctrination.org

A website where students can post comments about college courses and professors who engage in "thought reform" and "group think." You can search the site by school name.

www.thefire.org

Foundation for Individual Rights in Education (FIRE) describes itself as "a nonprofit educational foundation devoted to free speech, individual liberty, religious freedom, the rights of conscience, legal equality, due process, and academic freedom on our nation's campuses." This is the place to go for news updates on free speech issues regarding colleges. Also the place to go if you find yourself in deep water and need legal help. FIRE pops up in the hottest places and helps settle free speech issues. A group to watch.

www.townhall.com

Townhall.com describes its site as: "The first truly interactive community on the Internet to bring Internet users, conservative public policy organizations, congressional staff, and political activists together under the broad umbrella of 'conservative' thoughts, ideas, and actions. Townhall.com is a one-stop mall of ideas in which people congregate to exchange, discuss, and disseminate the latest news and information from the conservative movement. Townhall.com is committed to inform, educate, and empower the public through this emerging electronic medium.

"Townhall.com believes our community is of value. An interactive, open, and honest debate of the issues within the conservative community will help us all in the fight against those who would sacrifice the individual and freedom for political gain and big government."

Townhall.com is a project of the Heritage Foundation. The editor is Jonathan Garthwaite. Townhall is must reading for any college student looking for news analysis. Great links that come in handy for research.

www.worldnetdaily.com

Another solid news website that is very cutting edge. Editor and CEO is Joseph Farah. Site features news and commentary by Christians and conservatives. Often carries college campus news items. Links to U.S. newspapers, foreign newspapers, and wire services.

www.yaf.org

Young America's Foundation, is an educational organization that sponsors speakers on campus and in the community, distributes books and studies, holds conferences and seminars, and provides students with scholarship assistance. Site has a good bookstore.

ON PAPER

Maybe it's because I grew up in a home where both parents have a journalism background, but from middle school on, I've read the newspaper. There were times it was only the funnies, but over the years I developed the newspaper habit. When I went to college, some of my friends found it funny that I read a daily newspaper everyday (not the campus paper, although that can be entertaining as well). I asked where they got their news from and one of them said, "Oh, if something important happens, I just sort of know it."

College coursework takes a lot of time, but you should try to keep up on the world around you. Christians have a stereotype of having their heads in the sand; the last thing we need to do is reinforce that. Know your world. Speaking of world, in addition to reading a daily newspaper, or at least reading news sites on-line, the best source of news events is *World* magazine. *World* is a news magazine written with a Christian perspective. The issues are often thematic and are very in-depth, yet there is always "The Buzz," hot news, hot quotes, brief descriptions, and analysis of current movies, books, and music. *World* magazine is worth the money and the time.

I've also found it helpful to keep at least one book around that I'm reading for pleasure in addition to organic chemistry. There's not a lot of time for personal reading, but once in a while a book just clicks and you know the time to read it is now. Other times, the best you can do is write the book down and tackle the list when you're out of school.

This is a list I've culled from my own library, books I'm hoping to get to eventually, and from lists provided by friends. It also includes books related to specific fields of study that were recommended by Christians working as professionals in those fields. You can read more reviews on these books by going to www.amazon.com or going directly to the website of the publishing house. Publishing sites often offer a chapter or two for reading on-line.

Apologetics

Burden of Truth: Defending the Truth in an Age of Unbelief, Charles Colson (Tyndale, 1998)

This book consists of a brilliant collection of transcripts from Charles Colson's "BreakPoint" radio program, covering medical ethics, education, crime, science, pop culture, family, art, and government. Commentary points to the truth that the most fundamental dimension to human life is religious in nature. A helpful book for understanding difficult issues which sometimes collide with faith.

Christian Apologetics in a Postmodern World, edited by Timothy R. Phillips and Dennis L. Okholm (InterVarsity, 1995)

From the publisher: "Evangelicals are beginning to provide analyses of our postmodern society, but little has been done to suggest an effective apologetic strategy for reaching a culture that is pluralistic, consumer-oriented, and infatuated with managerial and therapeutic approaches to life. This, then, is the first book to address that vital task.

"In these pages some of evangelicalism's most stimulating thinkers consider three possible apologetic responses to post-modernity. William Lane Craig argues that traditional evidentialist apologetics remains viable and preferable. Roger Lundin, Nicola Creegan, and James Sire find the postmodern critique of Christianity and Western culture more challenging, but reject central features of it. Philip Kenneson, Brian Walsh, and J. Richard Middleton, on the other hand, argue that key aspects of postmodernity can be appropriated to defend orthodox Christianity.

"An essential feature are trenchant chapters by Ronald Clifton Potter, Dennis Hollinger, and Douglas Webster, considering issues facing the local church in light of postmodernity. The volumes' editors and John Stackhouse also add important introductory essays that orient the reader to postmodernity and various apologetic strategies.

"All this makes for a book indispensable for theologians, a wide range of students, and reflective pastors."

Christianity and Liberalism, by J. Gresham Machen (Eerdmans, 1946)

The age of this one makes it a classic. From the publisher: "Machen's classic defense of orthodox Christianity established the importance of scriptural doctrine and contrasts the teachings of liberalism and orthodoxy on God and man, the Bible, Christ, salvation, and the church. Though originally published nearly 70 years ago, the book maintains its relevance today."

How to Win the Culture War: A Christian Battle Plan for a Society in Crisis, by Peter Kreeft (InterVarsity Press, 2002)

Peter Kreeft is professor of philosophy at Boston College and author of numerous books. Kreeft describes the culture war, details who the real enemy is, and gives suggestions on how to wage war. The book has spunk — might have a little too much "attitude" for some.

Mere Christianity, C.S. Lewis (Harper San Francisco, 2001)

This is a classic. A good one to read while still in high school. You'll glean good theology and find out if you are or are not a C.S. Lewis fan.

From the publisher: "A forceful and accessible discussion of Christian belief that has become one of the most popular introductions to Christianity and one of the most popular of Lewis's books. Uncovers common ground upon which all Christians can stand together."

Mind Siege: The Battle for Truth in the New Millenium, by Tim LaHaye and David Noebel (Word Publishing, 2001)

From the publisher: "*New York Times* best-selling author Tim La-Haye and author David Noebel give a wake-up call for Christians to fight the tide of popular beliefs and win the battle for your mind. Two basic sources of reasoning determine the thoughts, ideas, beliefs, values, aims, morals, lifestyles, and activities of mankind — the wisdom of man and the wisdom of God. According to Tim LaHaye and David Noebel, life is mainly about the battle for your mind: whether you will live by man's wisdom, from the likes of Marx, Darwin, Freud, and Nietzsche, or God's wisdom and those who gave it, such as Moses, the prophets, Christ, and the Apostles. Your choice will affect the way you live now and ultimately where you will spend eternity."

Orthodoxy, by G.K. Chesterton (Ignatius Press, reprint, 1995)

From the publisher: "A timeless argument for traditional Christianity. If you think orthodoxy is boring and predictable, think again. In this timeless classic, G.K. Chesterton, one of the literary giants of the 20th century, presents a logical and personal reasoning for Christianity in model apologetic form. Gilbert Keith Chesterton was a self-described pagan at age 12 and totally agnostic by age 16. Yet, his spiritual journey ultimately led to a personal philosophy of orthodox, biblical Christianity. The account of his experiences, *Orthodoxy*, bridges the centuries and appeals to today's readers who face the same challenges of materialism, self-centeredness, and progress. Through philosophy, poetry, reason, and humor, Chesterton leads us on a literary journey toward truth."

Persecution, by David Limbaugh (Regnery, 2003)

David Limbaugh is the brother of radio talk-show host Rush Limbaugh. David is a strong and articulate Christian. *Persecution* is a heavily footnoted read and well researched. The book is a comprehensive analysis of the suppression of speech going on in schools, legal institutions, and the culture at large in the name of "tolerance." An engaging read.

From the publisher: "Tolerance might be the highest virtue in our popular culture, but it doesn't often extend to Christians these days. Christians are increasingly being driven from public life, denied their First Amendment rights, and even actively discriminated against for their beliefs. In this relentless exposé of political correctness run amok, best-selling author David Limbaugh rips apart the liberal hypocrisy that condones selective mistreatment of Christians in the mainstream media, Hollywood, our schools and universities, and throughout our public life."

The Abolition of Man, by C.S. Lewis (Harper San Francisco, 2001)

From the publisher: "C.S. Lewis sets out to persuade his audience of the importance and relevance of universal values such as courage and honor in contemporary society."

ARTS

A History of Western Music, by Donald Grout (W.W. Norton & Co., 2000)

Book description: "Recognized as the finest survey of Western art music in the English language, this distinguished book has enlightened a multitude of music lovers since it first appeared in 1960. This handsome new edition incorporates the latest advances in music scholarship."

Art and the Bible, by Francis Schaeffer (InterVarsity Press, 1973)

A short work that gives insight into understanding the beauty found in what today's artists are producing.

Dance Me a Story: Twelve Stories from the Classical Ballets, by Jane Rosenberg (Hudson Annex, 1993)

Wonderfully written and illustrated by Jane Rosenberg, this children's book (which is also appropriate and informative for adults wishing to learn more about classical ballet) features 12 tales from the classic ballets including Cinderella, Coppelia, Don Quixote, La Fille Mal Gardee, Firebird, Giselle, The Nutcracker, Petrouchka, Romeo and Juliet, The Sleeping Beauty, Swan Lake, and La Sylphide. The book provides information about the music and choreographers of these.

Letter of His Holiness Pope John Paul II to Artists, 1999

The link is incredibly long, so just Google it. This is fascinating reading for any student interested in any form of art. Even if you just go see movies, read it.

Sing Me a Story: The Metropolitan Opera's Book of Opera Stories for Children, by Jane Rosenberg, Luciano Pavarotti (Thames and Hudson, 1989)

This is a children's book, but excellent and easier to digest than most condensed opera libretto books. Tells the stories behind 15 operas — classic, modern, familiar, and those not so familiar. Jane Rosenberg brings her talents as a writer and illustrator, along with her passion and love for opera to this marvelous collection. Narratives are engaging, full of history, mystery, drama, humor and adventure. This may be a children's book, but it is really for both the young and the old.

State of the Arts: From Bezalel to Mapplethorpe, by Gene Edward Veith Jr. (Crossway, 1991)

From the publisher: "We cannot escape the arts. They permeate our lives and our culture — the décor, architecture, music, entertainment, everyday utensils. The imagination of this age, its ideas and concerns, percolate throughout the culture via the arts. These ideas affect us for good or for evil. The choice is not whether to live with art; we must choose whether to live with good art or bad art. Art — like all things human — needs to be redeemed. Christians cannot abandon the arts to the secular world, but can use them to display God's glory. This book will help us develop an informed artistic taste, open yet critical, discerning yet appreciative of what is truly excellent."

"*State of the Arts* wisely steers Christians between the two extremes of accepting inane cultural trends or dismissing all cultural pursuits as worldly. The book establishes a strong biblical context for understanding expressions of human creativity and powerfully defends art as a gift from God. Here is a much-needed counterattack on the aesthetic terrorism by entrenched enemies on the true, the good, and the beautiful." — Ken Myers, author of *All God's Children and Blue Suede Shoes.*

The Norton Anthology of Western Music, by Claude V. Palisca, editor (W.W. Norton & Co., 2001)

Book description: "From Adam (de la Halle) to Zwilich (Ellen), *The Norton Anthology of Western Music* provides a comprehensive collection of scores illustrating every significant trend, genre, and national school. These authoritative readings are reproduced from reliable and easy-to-read originals, and all foreign-language texts are accompanied by English translations. Each work in the anthology is discussed in *A History of Western Music*. The editor's notes and comments follow the score of each work.

"The new Fourth Edition includes 22 new selections, including works by Luca Marenzio, Benjamin Britten, Amy Beach, John Adams, and Ellen Taaffe Zwilich, all of whom are newly represented in *The Norton Anthology of Western Music*. (There is also a recorded version.)"

CHRISTIANS AT COLLEGE

Becoming a Contagious Christian, by Bill Hybels and Mark Mittelberg (Zondervan, 1996)

This is a good book, full of practical examples and solid thinking behind the whys and hows of sharing your faith.

From the publisher: "Evangelism doesn't have to be frustrating or intimidating. Bill Hybels and Mark Mittelberg believe that effectively communicating our faith in Christ should be the most natural thing in the world. We just need encouragement and direction. In *Becoming a Contagious Christian*, Hybels and Mittelberg articulate the central principles that have helped the believers at Willow Creek Community Church become a church known around the world for its outstanding outreach to unchurched people. Based on the words of Jesus and flowing from the firsthand experiences of the authors, *Becoming a Contagious Christian* is a groundbreaking, personalized approach to relational evangelism. You will discover your own natural evangelism style, how to develop a contagious

Christian character, to build spiritually strategic relationships, to direct conversations toward matters of faith, and to share biblical truths in everyday language. This landmark book presents a blueprint for starting a spiritual epidemic of hope and enthusiasm for spreading the gospel."

Celebration of Discipline: The Path to Spiritual Growth, by Richard Foster (Harper San Francisco, 1988)

From the publisher: "Hailed by many as the best modern book on Christian spirituality, *Celebration of Discipline* explores the 'classic disciplines,' or central spiritual practices, of the Christian faith. Along the way, Foster shows that it is only by and through these practices that the true path to spiritual growth can be found.

"Dividing the disciplines into three movements of the Spirit, Foster shows how each of these areas contribute to a balanced spiritual life. The inward disciplines of meditation, prayer, fasting, and study, offer avenues of personal examination and change. The outward disciplines of simplicity, solitude, submission, and service, help prepare us to make the world a better place. The corporate disciplines of confession, worship, guidance, and celebration, bring us nearer to one another and to God."

Finding Common Ground: How to Communicate With Those Outside the Christian Community . . . While We Still Can, by Tim Downs (Moody, 1999)

I've heard so many people rave about this book, and after reading it, now wish I'd read it *before* college instead of *in* college. The author builds a case that Christians are so intent on harvesting that we neglect the business of sowing. He also addresses the direct versus the indirect method of showing truth. This approach doesn't always work in a classroom situation, but is thought-provoking and practical for other arenas of life.

How to Stay Christian in College: An Interactive Guide to Keeping the Faith, by J. Budziszewski (NavPress, 1999)

We must have three or four copies of this floating around home. My siblings and I were given a copy by our parents and we have loaner copies as well. This book is excellent for the high school senior. It gives a topic-by-topic look at what to expect. Some of it will be a review for mature Christians, but it never hurts to hear the truth one more time.

From the publisher: "Going to college usually means leaving behind your network of support and heading to a world with different perspectives, responsibilities, and expectations. Even if you're going to a 'Christian' college, there's no guarantee you won't face challenges to your faith. . . . So how *do* you stay Christian in college? How do you stay open about your faith in the face of potential ridicule? *How to Stay Christian in College* is an interactive guide through the maze of college realities. J. Budziszewski discusses the foundations of the Christian faith and directly addresses different world views and myths that students encounter at college. Filled with quotes, statistics, resources, stories, and encouragement, it will equip you to conquer the dangers that lie ahead."

DIVERSITY, TOLERANCE, AND INTOLERANCE

Letters to a Young Conservative, by Dinesh D'Souza (Basic Books, 2002)

I dog-eared this one. My roommate read it, my brother read it. It's a great book for anyone heading to or already on a secular campus. It was solid, informative, encouraging, entertaining, and uplifting. (Parents enjoy this book, too!) The book is a series of letter responses to a young conservative who asks questions about all the hot-button issues. D'Souza, along with Ben Hart, was also one of the founders of the *Dartmouth Review* at Dartmouth University. *Letters to a Young Conservative* offers great advice to students today. The book is upbeat and encouraging and filled with humor.

Poisoned Ivy, by Benjamin Hart (Stein and Day Publishers, 1984)

This book is out of print; you'll have to find it on www. half. com or other sites. The book details the onset of the liberal *ethos* at Dartmouth in the early 1980s. Reading it 20 years after the fact is like reading about the labor and delivery of the PC movement. Hart and his buddies did their best to turn the administration on its ear, including starting the *Dartmouth Review*. Some of the things they did back then could possibly get you arrested today. Good narrative, great stories. You'll recognize a lot of names that were in the hotbed of the conservative movement, as students back then are still at the head of the pack today, 25 years later.

The New Tolerance, by Josh McDowell and Bob Hostetler (Tyndale House, 1998)

The authors analyze what they refer to as the "new tolerance." The book also contains biblical strategy for countering the "new tolerance."

From the publisher: "This book will help readers discern truth from error and to withstand the pressure — even persecution — to conform to a relativistic culture."

The Shadow University: The Betrayal of Liberty on America's Campuses, by Alan Charles Kors and Harvey A. Silvergate (Perennial, 1999)

This book takes a look at the state of college campuses through the lenses of two hard-core civil libertarians. They document the assault on liberty, individualism, dignity, and due process that runs unchecked on many campuses today. This is a compelling narrative regarding the current state of indoctrination. The book is passionate and the passion is contagious. A little on the dry and detailed side, but it is considered a classic on the topic of college and indoctrination.

ECONOMICS

CHRISTIANS IN THE MARKETPLACE:

1. *Biblical Principles and Public Policy: The Practice* (Christians in the Marketplace Series, Vol. 4), by Richard B. Chewning (NavPress 1991)

2. *Biblical Principles and Business: The Practice* (Christians in the Marketplace Series, Vol. 3), by Richard Chewning (NavPress 1990)

3. *Biblical Principles and Business: The Foundations* (Christians in the Marketplace Series), by Richard Chewning (NavPress 1989)

4. *Biblical Principles and Economics: The Foundations* (Christians in the Marketplace Series), by Richard Chewning (NavPress 1989)

From reviewer Brian Burnett: "Most of the chapters in the books are written by theologians, philosophers, and historians. Given that, the chapters have been written for average people rather than for theologians and philosophers. The scholars selected to work on the theological foundations books were chosen on three grounds: (1) they all have a very high view of Scripture as the authoritative Word of God, (2) they are representative leaders from different theological schools, thus their methods and systems of biblical interpretation offer an orthodox but creative range, and (3) their assigned topics fit their demonstrated interests.

"In summary, when I was preparing to teach in Russia, these are the only books I found after an exhaustive search that gave true biblical foundations for developing a perspective on economics and business."

Transforming Charity: Toward a Results-oriented Social Sector, by Ryan Streeter (economics) (Hudson Institute, 2001)

Reviewer Don Eberly, deputy director of the White House Office for Faith Based and Community Initiatives and deputy assistant to the president: "Charities are becoming market-oriented; faith-based organizations are engaging in civic initiatives; social innovators are turning charitable gifts into investments; and the social sector is growing more complex as local communities find new ways to address the needs of those left behind. In *Transforming Charity*, Hudson Institute's Ryan Streeter examines the developing trend to assist those in need in ways that deliver real results by changing lives and changing how charity is practiced. He works with concrete examples and draws connections to the larger movement in America to strengthen the institutions of civil society. *Transforming Charity* is a book fit for an age that is both coping with the forces of devolution and experiencing a renewed confidence in local communities' ability to help their fellow citizens.

"In *Transforming Charity*, Streeter surveys the rapidly expanding movement to the social sector as a place where community problems can be effectively confronted. Streeter offers fresh evidence to suggest that there is a holistic form of charity that holds enormous promise for transforming people's lives. *Transforming Charity*'s timely release will clearly help shape a new direction in social policy in Washington."

EDUCATION

Classical Education: The Movement Sweeping America (Studies in Philanthropy), by Gene Edward Veith Jr. and Andrew Kern (Capital Research Center, 2001)

From the publisher: "*Classical Education* examines the decline of American education and offers a solution. It's not more spending or a new and innovative program. The solution, according to authors Gene Edward Veith Jr. and Andrew Kern, is classical education."

Created to Learn: A Christian Teacher's Introduction to Educational Psychology, by William R. Yount (Broadman and Holman, 1996)

From the publisher: "Chapter one establishes a seven-fold approach — the Disciplers' Model to Christian teaching. This model was developed in response to a question that would not let the author go: 'How should I teach so that my learners will grow in the Lord?' "

The Dictionary of Cultural Literacy: What Every American Needs to Know, by James Trefil, Joseph F. Kett, and E.D. Hirsch Jr., editors (Houghton Mifflin, 2002)

This book is an absolute must have!

Book description: "In this fast-paced information age, how can Americans know what's really important and what's just a passing fashion? Now more than ever, we need a source that concisely sums up the knowledge that matters to Americans — the people, places, ideas, and events that shape our cultural conversation. With more than six thousand entries, *The Dictionary of Cultural Literacy* is that invaluable source.

"Wireless technology. Gene therapy. NAFTA. In addition to the thousands of terms described in the original Dictionary of Cultural Literacy, here are more than five hundred new entries to bring Americans' bank of essential knowledge up to date. The original entries have been fully revised to reflect recent changes in world history and politics, American literature, and, especially, science and technology. Cultural icons that have stood the test of time (Odysseus, Leaves of Grass, Cleopatra, the Taj Mahal, D-Day) appear alongside entries on such varied concerns as cryptography, the digital divide, the European Union, Kwanzaa, pheromones, SPAM, Type A and Type B personalities, Web browsers, and much, much more."

The Devil Knows Latin: Why America Needs the Classical Tradition, by E. Christian Kopff (Intercollegiate Studies Institute, 2001)

From the publisher: "*The Devil Knows Latin* is a provocative and illuminating examination of contemporary American culture. Its range is broad and fascinating. Whether discussing the importance of Greek and Latin syntax to our society, examining current trends in literary theory, education, and politics, or applying a classical perspective to contemporary films, Christian Kopff (professor of classics at the University of Colorado) is at home and on the mark. He outlines the perils and possibilities for America in the coming decades with learning and verve — demonstrating that the highway to a creative and free future begins as a Roman road."

The Seven Laws of Teaching, by John Milton Gregory (Baker Book House, 1995)

From the publisher: "John Milton Gregory's clear and concise presentation of the fundamental laws of teaching has been studied and applied in a variety of educational situations, from church schools to in-service programs of prestigious businesses. For generations, teachers have benefited from the solid advice in this book.

"The frequent reprintings of this classic work, first published in 1884, testify to the timelessness of its contents. Educational fads come and go, but the basic principles of teaching and learning, those discussed in this book, are not subject to the winds of change."

The Well-Educated Mind: A Guide to the Classical Education You Never Had, by Susan Wise Bauer (W.W. Norton & Company, 2003)

From the publisher: "An engaging, accessible guide to educating yourself in the classical tradition. Surrounded by more books than ever, readers today are frequently daunted by the classics they have left unread. *The Well-Educated Mind*, debunking our own inferiority complexes, is a wonderful resource for anyone wishing to explore and develop the mind's capacity to read and comprehend the 'greatest hits' in fiction, autobiography, history, poetry, and drama."

Recovering the Lost Tools of Education: An Approach to Distinctively Christian Education, by Douglas Wilson (Good News Pub., 1991)

From the publisher: "Public education is in crisis. At the heart of the problem is the idea that education can exist in a moral vacuum. Describes the melee in public education and calls for a return to classical teaching methods.

"Public education in America has run into hard times. Even many within the system admit that it is failing. While many factors contribute, Douglas Wilson lays much blame on the idea that education can take place in a moral vacuum. It is not possible for education to be nonreligious, deliberately excluding the basic questions about life. All education builds on the foundation of someone's world view. Education deals with fundamental questions that require religious answers. Learning to read and write is simply the process of acquiring the tools to ask and answer such questions.

"A second reason for the failure of public schools, Wilson feels, is modern teaching methods. He argues for a return to a classical education, firm discipline, and the requirement of hard work.

"Often educational reforms create new problems that must be solved down the road. This book presents alternatives that have proved workable in experience."

You Can't Get a Good Education . . . If They're Only Telling You Half the Story (Campaign for Fairness and Inclusion in Higher Education)

Excellent booklet that documents the biases on college campuses. Available through the Center for the Study of Popular Culture, (800) 752-6562.

FILM

Finding God in the Movies: 33 Films of Reel Faith, by Robert K. Johnston and Catherine M. Barsotti (Baker Book House, 2004)

This book analyzes biblical concepts in contemporary films. A good book for those interested in film and a good book for opening the door to discussion with non-Christian friends.

From the publisher: "Almost everyone goes to the movies
— including Christians. Recognizing this, the authors present a unique resource to help believers engage and enjoy films of faith. Included are resources for understanding and discerning the Christian message relevant to 33 recent movies now available in video or

DVD formats. This unique book examines topics such as racial reconciliation, forgiveness, and service through films such as *Planet of the Apes; Billy Elliot; Life is Beautiful; The Truman Show;* and *Crouching Tiger, Hidden Dragon.*

Hollywood Worldviews, Watching Films With Wisdom & Discernment, by Brian Godawa (InterVarsity Press, 2002)

From the publisher: "Do you watch movies with your eyes open?

"You buy your tickets and concessions, and you walk into the theater. Celluloid images flash at twenty-four frames per second, and the hypnotic sequence of moving pictures coaxes you to suspend disbelief and be entertained by the implausible.

"Unfortunately, many often suspend their beliefs as well, succumbing to subtle lessons in how to behave, think, and even perceive reality. Do you find yourself hoping that a sister will succeed in seducing her sibling's husband, that a thief will get away with his crime, that a serial killer will escape judgment? Do you, too, laugh at the bumbling priest and seethe at the intolerant and abusive evangelist? Do you embrace worldviews that infect your faith and wonder, after your head is clear, whether your faith can survive the infection?

"Brian Godawa guides you through the place of redemption in film, the tricks screenwriters use to communicate their messages, and the mental and spiritual discipline required for watching movies. *Hollywood Worldviews* helps you enter a dialogue with Hollywood that leads to a happier ending, one that keeps you aware of your culture and awake to your faith."

HISTORY

America's Real War, by Daniel Lapin, (Multnomah, 1999)

From the publisher: "There is a tug of war going on for the future of America. At one end of the rope are those who think America is a secular nation; at the other are those who believe religion is at the root of our country's foundation. In *America's Real War*, renowned leader and speaker Rabbi Daniel Lapin argues that America was founded in a Judeo-Christian tradition and that the tradition is essential to restoring the country to tranquility, spiritual vitality, and moral greatness. With his thorough knowledge of Christianity, history, political theory, and business, Rabbi Lapin gives a sound defense for Christianity as the backbone of our society, maintains that our best days lie ahead of us — and provides a road map for getting us there."

The History of the English Speaking Peoples (**4 volumes**), by Winston Churchill (Dodd Mead)

The Patriot's Handbook, by George Grant (Cumberland House, 1996)

From the publisher: "British philosopher G.K. Chesterton once quipped that America is the only nation ever founded on a creed. While other nations find their identity in geography, culture, ideology, or ethnic origin, America was founded on certain ideas about freedom, human dignity, and social responsibility.

"Early in the 19th century, American educators began to realize that if this great experiment in liberty was to be maintained, then an informed patriotism would have to be instilled in the young. The ideals that produced the nation needed to pass from one generation to the next; thus, these educators presented rising new citizens with a small handbook containing the essential elements of the American creed.

"*The Patriot's Handbook* is a 21st-century version of that tradition. A concise introduction to the ideas, events, and personalities of American freedom, it is a valuable resource for anyone who wishes to understand the nation's identity as it has developed from its founding until now. Included are key documents — for example, the Mayflower Compact, the Declaration of Independence, the Federalist Papers — speeches, poems, song lyrics, and profiles of the presidents and many of the leaders who have shaped the nation's history."

The Roots of American Order, by Russell Kirk (Intercollegiate Studies Institute, 2004)

From the publisher: "What holds America together? In this classic work, Russell Kirk describes the beliefs and institutions that have nurtured the American soul and commonwealth. Beginning with the Hebrew prophets, Kirk examines in dramatic fashion the sources of American order. His analytical narrative might be called 'a tale of five cities': Jerusalem, Athens, Rome, London, and Philadelphia. For an understanding of the significance of America at the dawn of a new century, Russell Kirk's masterpiece on the history of American civilization is unsurpassable. This edition includes a new foreword by the distinguished historian Forrest McDonald."

Turning Points, Decisive Moments in the History of Christianity, by Mark Noll (Baker Books, 2000)

What's So Great About America, by Dinesh D'Souza (Regnery Publishing, 2002)

A marvelous primer on conservatism and America written by a first-generation American with a great mind and sharp wit. Has a lot of the info you should have learned in history and civics, but might have missed. His perspective makes you appreciate the freedoms and liberty we Americans have taken for granted.

Worldly Saints — The Puritans as They Really Were, by Leland Ryken (Zondervan, 1986)

Dr. Ryken's presentation of the Puritan view and style of life is perceptive and accurate. He allows the Puritans to speak for themselves on topics ranging from "church and worship" to "money" and "marriage and sex.

LITERATURE

Best Loved Poems of the American People, by Hazel Felleman (Doubleday reissue, 1936)

From the publisher: "More than 1,500,000 copies in print! Over 575 traditional favorites to be read and reread. Categorized by theme, and indexed by author and first line, this is a collection that will be treasured."

Brightest Heaven of Invention: A Christian Guide to Six Shakespeare Plays, by Peter Leithart (Canon Press, 1996)

From the publisher: "Shakespeare was a great observer who was able to see into the patterns of human character. Dare anyone say that these insights are irrelevant to living in the real world? For many in an older generation, the Bible and the Collected Shakespeare were the two indispensable books. Leithart's perceptive walk through these plays is written especially for a high-school level course, but older students will benefit as well. The six plays discussed are: *Henry V, Julius Caesar, Hamlet, Macbeth, The Taming of the Shrew,* and *Much Ado About Nothing.*

Hinds' Feet on High Places, by Hannah Hurnard (Tyndale, 1997)

From the publisher: "*Hinds' Feet on High Places* is one of Hannah Hurnard's best known and best loved books. This book is a beautiful allegory dramatizing the yearning of God's children to be led to new heights of love, joy, and victory. Follow Much-Afraid on her spiritual journey through difficult places with her two companions, Sorrow and Suffering. Learn how Much-Afraid overcomes her tormenting fears as she passes through many dangers and mounts at last to the High Places. There she gains a new name and returns to her valley of service, transformed by her union with the loving Shepherd."

How to Read Slowly, by James W. Sire (Shaw, 1988)

From the publisher: "Your eyes see the words, but do you read what you see? Every article, poem, book, even every printed advertisement not only carries information but also projects a way of looking at life. In *How to Read Slowly*, James Sire helps readers detect not only what writers say but what lies behind what they say.

"The careful reading of any book requires that we seek out the author's standpoint. What is the author's larger philosophical commitment? What does he or she think life is about? Any book, fiction, or prose should be sifted, probed, and it's world view exposed. Slowing down will increase our comprehension.

"*How to Read*, now in its third edition, has been used in higher education classroom to teach reading comprehension."

How to Read the Bible for All Its Worth, by Gordon D. Fee and Douglas Stuart (Zondervan, 2003)

From the publisher: "Understanding the Bible isn't for the few, the gifted, the scholarly. The Bible is accessible. It's meant to be read and comprehended by everyone from armchair readers to seminary students. A few essential insights into the Bible can clear up a lot of misconceptions and help you grasp the meaning of Scripture and its application to your 21st-century life.

"Covering everything from translational concerns to different genres of biblical writing, *How to Read the Bible for All Its Worth* is used all around the world. In clear, simple language, it helps you accurately understand the different parts of the Bible — their meaning for ancient audiences and their implications for you today — so you can uncover the inexhaustible worth that is in God's Word."

Realms of Gold: The Classics in Christian Perspective, by Leland Ryken (Wipf & Stock Publishers, 2003)

From the publisher: "In *Realms of Gold*, Leland Ryken proceeds chronologically through some of the best of the best, from Homer through Shakespeare to Camus, offering not only a taste of the classics, but a framework in which to analyze them.

"For students studying literature, this book serves as an introduction to the classics as friends; for those who have not read the classics in a long time, it is motivation to renew delightful acquaintances; for people who already know the classics as intimate friends, it offers the opportunity to renew acquaintance within a Christian context."

Screwtape Letters, by C.S. Lewis (Harper San Francisco, 1942)

From the publisher: "In this humorous and perceptive exchange between two devils, C.S. Lewis delves into moral questions about good versus evil, temptation, repentance, and grace. Through this wonderful tale, the reader emerges with a better understanding of what it means to live a faithful life."

The Complete Works of William Shakespeare, by William Shakespeare

The Devil's Race-Track: Mark Twain's Great Dark Writings, edited by John S. Tuckey (University of California Press, 1966, 1972, 1980)

From the publisher: "Mark Twain explores the darker side of life in these little-known later writings. The tone is lightened considerably by Twain's sagely ironic humor that balances his tough-mindedness."

This book should be used as an apologetic discussion.

MEDIA AND CULTURE

All God's Children and Blue Suede Shoes: Christians & Popular Culture, by Ken Myers (Crossway, 2003)

The author takes a hard and sometimes amusing look at pop culture. Myers gives his research a theological framework. His insights are timely, fresh, and relevant.

Amusing Ourselves to Death: Public Discourse in the Age of Show Business, by Neil Postman (Penguin, 1985)

From the publisher: "Television has conditioned us to tolerate visually entertaining material measured out in spoonfuls of time, to the detriment of rational public discourse and reasoned public affairs. In this eloquent, persuasive book, Neil Postman alerts us to the real and present dangers of this state of affairs, and offers compelling suggestions as to how to withstand the media onslaught. Before we hand over politics, education, religion, and journalism to the show business demands of the television age, we must recognize the ways in which the media shape our lives and the ways we can, in turn, shape them to serve our highest goals.

Fit Bodies, Fat Minds: Why Evangelicals Don't Think and What to Do About It, by Os Guinness (Baker Books, 1994)

From the publisher: "The author traces the dumbing down of evangelicalism as it has accommodated itself to popular culture. He sees a deepening anti-intellectualism that has become a crippling cultural handicap."

Redeeming Pop Culture: A Kingdom Approach, by T.M. Moore (P & R Press, 2003)

T.M. Moore is an easy-to-read writer that stirs the pot. In this book he describes the "kudzu" of popular culture (kudzu refers to a vine that spreads like crazy and easily grows out of control). Moore's critique has a sound theological base.

From the publisher: "Helps us understand popular culture, which confronts and challenges us daily. Fosters an appreciation of this phenomenon without compromising our calling to seek first God's kingdom."

Remote Control, by Carl Kerby (Master Books, 2006)

From the publisher: "Hollywood has a world view — if you are only checking for ratings, you're missing a whole other level of humanism and anti-Christianity that is being slipped quietly and unobtrusively into your entertainment choices. Kerby cites example after example of the 'evolutionizing of the American culture,' pointing out Darwinian references not only in present-day television and movies, but in some "old classics" as well. The cumulative effect is a remarkable and dangerous one — which impacts and may even undermine the biblical truths you hope to instill in your family. Break Hollywood's grip — and get tuned into its real agenda."

Seinfeld and Philosophy: A Book about Everything and Nothing, edited by William Irwin (Open Court Publishing, 1999)

This is part of a *Popular Culture and Philosophy* series.

From the publisher: "How is Jerry like Socrates? Is it rational for George to 'do the opposite?' Would Simone de Beauvoir say that Elaine is a feminist? Is Kramer stuck in Kierkegaard's aesthetic stage? *Seinfeld and Philosophy* is both an enlightening look at the most popular sitcom of the 1990s and an entertaining introduction to philosophy via Seinfeld's plots and characters. These 14 essays, which explore the ideas of Plato, Aristotle, Lao-Tzu, Heidegger, Kant, Marx, Kierkegaard, Nietzsche, Sartre, and Wittgenstein, will show readers how to be masters of their philosophical domain."

The Consequences of Ideas: Understanding the Concepts that Shaped our World, by R.C. Sproul (Crossway Books, 2000)

From the publisher: "To understand our culture today, we need to be familiar with the ideas that have shaped it. From ancient Greek thinkers like Plato and Aristotle to Christian philosophers Augustine and Aquinas to the molders of modern thought such as Kant and Nietzsche, R.C. Sproul demonstrates the consequences their ideas have had on world events, theology, and our everyday lives — for better or for worse — and challenges us to respond from a Christian perspective."

The Scandal of the Evangelical Mind, Mark A. Noll (W.B. Eerdmans Publishing Company, 1995)

From the publisher: "The scandal of the evangelical mind is that there is not much of an evangelical mind." So begins this award-winning intellectual history and critique of the evangelical movement by one of evangelicalism's most respected historians.

"Unsparing in his judgment, Mark Noll ask why the largest single group of religious Americans — who enjoy increasing wealth, status, and political influence — have contributed so little to rigorous intellectual scholarship in North America. In nourishing believers in the simple truths of the gospel, why have evangelicals failed at sustaining a serious intellectual life and abandoned the universities, the arts, and other realms of 'high' culture?

"Noll is probing and forthright in his analysis of how this situation came about, but he doesn't end there. Challenging the evangelical community, he sets out to find, within evangelicalism itself, resources for turning the situation around."

PHILOSOPHY

A God of Suffering? DVD by Dr. Tommy Mitchell (Answers in Genesis)

From the publisher:: "In the wake of natural disasters and human-engineered tragedy, everyone is asking how a loving God could allow this evil to happen. Biblical answers and insight lay a strong foundation for belief in God."

Christianity and Western Thought: A History of Philosophers, Ideas and Movements, by Colin Brown (InterVarsity Press, 1990)

From the publisher: "Colin Brown provides a sweeping survey of Christianity and Western thought from the ancient world to the Age of Enlightenment. Students, pastors, and thoughtful Christians will benefit from this rich source that sketches the history of philosophers, ideas, and movements that have influenced and been influenced by Christian thought. From Socrates and the Sophists to Kant, from Augustine to Aquinas and the Reformers, Brown tells the often tension-filled story of the people and ideas that have shaped our intellectual landscape. Is philosophy the 'handmaiden of faith' or 'the doctrine of demons'? Does it clarify the faith or undermine the very heart of what Christians believe?"

Desiring God, by John Piper (Multnomah, 2003)

From the publisher: "Scripture reveals that the great business of life is to glorify God by enjoying Him forever. In this paradigm-shattering classic, newly revised and expanded, John Piper reveals that the debate between duty and delight doesn't truly exist: Delight is our duty. Readers will embark on a dramatically different and joyful experience of their faith."

Escape from Reason, by Francis Schaeffer (InterVarsity Fellowship, 1968)

Schaeffer lays out the "line of despair" separating the realms of supernatural and natural.

How Should We Then Live: The Rise and Decline of Western Thought and Culture, by Francis Schaeffer (Good News Pub, 1983)

Schaeffer, a man many regard as one of the greatest Christian philosophers of the 20th century, traces the development of ideas and the consequences of ideas throughout Western civilization beginning with Rome and ending with the post-modern world. A classic.

How Now Shall We Live? by Charles Colson and Nancy Pearcey (Tyndale, 1999)

From the publisher: "Christianity is more than a personal relationship with Jesus Christ. It is also a world view that not only answers life's basic questions — Where did we come from, and who are we? What has gone wrong with the world? What can we do to fix it? — but also shows us how we should live as a result of those answers. *How Now Shall We Live?* gives Christians the understanding, the confidence, and the tools to confront the world's bankrupt world views and to restore and redeem every aspect of contemporary culture: family, education, ethics, work, law, politics, science, art, music. This book will change every Christian who reads it. It will change the Church in the new millennium."

How to Think About the Great Ideas (from the Great Books of Western Civilization), by Mortimer J. Adler, edited by Max Weismann (Open Court Publishing, 2000)

From the publisher: "In *How to Think about The Great Ideas,* Adler summarizes the most important ideas of Western thought, explicating their histories and developments as well as their importance in our lives today. He explains not only what the great ideas are, but why they are great. This volume is an excellent introduction to the key ideas of 2,500 years of Western thought."

Loving God With All Your Mind: Thinking as a Christian in the Postmodern World, by Gene Edward Veith Jr. (Crossway, 2003)

A good book by a prolific writer and thinker of our times. For students of all ages.

From the publisher: "How should Christians react to current intellectual thought and the new, often unsettling ideas that accompany it? Gene Edward Veith Jr. shows that Christians must address contemporary thinking — they cannot only grapple with new ideas without compromising their faith, but Christianity provides a superior basis for pursuing knowledge than do competing world views."

No Doubt About It, by Winfried Corduan, (Broadman and Holman, 1997)

From the publisher: "Our doubts and questions make us feel so faithless. But according to Dr. Winfried Corduan, the very thoughts that call our faith into question are actually signs of life and growth. 'We should never fear investigating the truth,' he writes. 'If we have to run from the truth, maybe it's because we have something to hide.' In this rigorous look at the essence of Christianity, Corduan argues from a compatibility between faith and reason."

Saint Thomas Aquinas, by G.K. Chesterton (House of Stratus, 2000)

The Consolation of Philosophy, by Anicius Boethius (Penguin Classic reissue, 2000)

Considered by C.S. Lewis as one of the ten most influential books in his life.

From the publisher: "Written in prison before his brutal execution in A.D. 524, Boethius's *The Consolation of Philosophy* is a conversation between the ailing prisoner and his 'nurse,' Philosophy, whose instruction restores him to health and brings him to enlightenment. Boethius was an eminent public figure who had risen to great political heights in the court of King Theodoric when he was implicated in conspiracy and condemned to death. Although a Christian, it was to the pagan Greek philosophers that he turned for inspiration following his abrupt fall from grace. With great clarity of thought and philosophical brilliance, Boethius adopted the classical model of the dialogue to debate the vagaries of Fortune, and to explore the nature of happiness, good and evil, fate and free will.

"Victor Watts's English translation makes *The Consolation of Philosophy* accessible to the modern reader while losing nothing of its poetic artistry and breadth of vision. This edition includes an introduction discussing Boethius's life and writings, a bibliography, glossary, and notes."

The Everlasting Man, G.K. Chesterton (Ignatius Press, 1993)

From the publisher: "This volume contains three of Chesterton's greatest classics on Catholic philosophy and spirituality. It includes *The Everlasting Man*, possibly his greatest work, which gives an incarnational view of world history, and two of the finest biographies written of St. Thomas and St. Francis."

The Problem of Pain, C.S. Lewis (Harper San Francisco, 2001)

From the publisher: "Why must humanity suffer? In this elegant and thoughtful work, C.S. Lewis questions the pain and suffering that occur everyday and how this contrasts with the notion of a God that is both omnipotent and good. An answer to this critical theological problem is found within these pages."

Time for Truth, Living Free in a World of Lies, Hype and Spin, by Os Guinness (Baker Book House, 2000)

From the publisher: "In our postmodern society, truth no longer exists in any objective or absolute sense. At best, truth is considered relative; at worst, a matter of human convention. But as Os Guinness points out in this important book, truth is a vital requirement for freedom and a good life.

"*Time for Truth* will challenge you to seek the truth, speak the truth, and live the truth. It will show you that becoming a free and truthful person is the deepest secret of integrity and the highest form of taking responsibility for yourself and for your life."

SCIENCE

Creation: Facts of Life, by Gary Parker (Master Books, 1994)

From the publisher: "Written by a former evolutionary biologist, *Creation: Facts of Life* examines the classic arguments for evolution as taught in public schools and universities, then refutes them in an easy-to-read style."

Darwin on Trial, by Phillip E. Johnson (InterVarsity Press, 1993)

From the publisher: "Here's the book that has rocked the scientific — and Christian — establishment. Phillip Johnson's critique of Darwinian evolution touched off explosions among scientists and theologians almost from the day of its publication in 1992. The volatile debate was at first carried on in academic journals and in magazines like *Nature* and *Scientific American.* It even engaged the attention of leading evolutionists like Nobel Laureate physicist Steven Weinberg and prominent naturalist Stephen Jay Gould. Johnson was invited to debate several of his opponents at universities across the country. And he was himself the subject of debate: Michael Ruse, author of *Darwinism Defended,* spoke at an annual meeting of the American Association for the Advancement of Science on the topic 'Nonliteralist Anti-Evolutionism: The Case of Phillip Johnson.'

"Clearly, Johnson's arguments have been taken seriously by Darwinists of every sort. And though at first the mainstream press seemed to be out of earshot (except for reviews in *Publisher's Weekly* and the *National Review*), news of *Darwin on Trial* eventually reached wider audiences. Last summer, Johnson appeared with William F. Buckley on *Firing Line*. And in May 1995 he was interviewed on the PBS telecast *In the Beginning: The Creationist Controversy with Randall Balmer*. These and other indications of expanding interest in his critique is good news for all who wish to bring the debate over Darwinism into the bright light of day."

Darwin's Black Box: The Biochemical Challenge to Evolution, by Michael J. Behe (Free Press, 1998)

From the publisher: "In *Darwin's Black Box,* Michael Behe argues that evidence of evolution's limits has been right under our noses — but it is so small that we have only recently been able to see it. The field of biochemistry, begun when Watson and Crick discovered the double-helical shape of DNA, has unlocked the secrets of the cell. There, biochemists have unexpectedly discovered a world of Lilliputian complexity. As Behe engagingly demonstrates, using the examples of vision, blood clotting, cellular transport, and more, the biochemical world comprises an arsenal of chemical machines, made up of finely calibrated, interdependent parts. For Darwinian evolution to be true, there must have been a series of mutations, each of which produced its own working machine, that led to the complexity we can now see. The more complex and interdependent each machine's parts are shown to be, the harder it is to envision Darwin's gradualistic paths. Behe surveys the professional science literature and shows that it is completely silent on the subject, stymied by the elegance of the foundation of life. Could it be that there is some greater force at work?

"Michael Behe is not a creationist. He believes in the scientific method, and he does not look to religious dogma for answers to these questions. But he argues persuasively that biochemical machines must have been *designed* — either by God, or by some other higher intelligence. For decades science has been frustrated, trying to reconcile the astonishing discoveries of modern biochemistry to a 19th-century theory that cannot accommodate them. With the publication of *Darwin's Black Box,* it is time for scientists to allow themselves to consider exciting new possibilities, and for the rest of us to watch closely."

From Evolution to Creation DVD by Gary Parker (Answers in Genesis)

From the publisher: "A respected biology professor explains his conversion from dogmatic belief in evolution to biblical creation. Warm, humble, and humorous, Dr. Parker shows how the Lord helped him to see the false assumptions."

The Soul of Science, by Nancy R. Pearcy and Charles B. Thaxton (Crossway Books, 1994)

From the publisher: "This 'Turning Point' book surveys the development of science and its historic and present relationship to Christianity, and re-introduces believers to their rich intellectual heritage."

The Wedge of Truth: Splitting the Foundations of Naturalism, by Phillip E. Johnson (InterVarsity Press, 2000)

From the publisher: "Science is the supreme authority in our culture. If there is a dispute, science arbitrates it. If a law is to be passed, science must ratify it. If truth is to be taught, science must approve it. And when science is ignored, storms of protest are heard in the media, in the university — even in local coffee shops.

"While we may learn a great deal from science, it does not offer us unlimited knowledge. In fact, most scientists readily acknowledge that science cannot provide answers to questions of ultimate purpose or meaning. So to what authority will we turn for these?

"The deficiencies in science and the philosophy (naturalism) that undergirds it call for a cognitive revolution — a fundamental change in our thinking habits. And it all begins with a wedge of truth.

"This wedge of truth does not 'wedge out' a necessary foundation of rational thought. But it does 'wedge in' the much-needed acknowledgment that reason encompasses more than mere scientific investigation. Phillip E. Johnson argues compellingly for an understanding of reason that brings scientific certainty back into relational balance with philosophical inquiry and religious faith.

"Applying his wedge of truth, Johnson analyzes the latest debates between science and religion played out in our media, our universities, and society at large. He looks to thinkers such as Newbigin, Polanyi, and Pascal to lay a foundation for our seeing the universe in a totally different way. And from that base he then considers the educational programs and research agendas that should be undertaken — and have already begun in some earnest — during this new century."

VIRTUE

A Return to Modesty: Discovering the Lost Virtue, by Wendy Shalit (Touchstone Books, 2000)

A book on the topic of modesty written by Shalit at the age of 23. She details her own experiences through grade school sex education, the discover of "modestyniks" — Orthodox Jewish women who withhold physical contact from men until marriage, and astute observations on modesty, eating disorders, and hooking up, that she gleaned while at Williams College. Excellent book — a must-read for every female.

WORLD VIEWS

Answering Islam: The Crescent in Light of the Cross, by Norman L. Geisler and Abdul Saleeb (Baker Book House, 2002)

Post 9/11, almost every college campus has worked Islam into a core freshman class. It's good to study world religions — the only thing is, you don't often get the full picture, let alone much depth. This book is helpful in grasping the full scope of Islam and examining the differences between Islam and Christianity. You won't get this in class.

From the publisher: "What are the fundamental beliefs of Islam and how can Christians respond to them? *Answering Islam* evaluates the claims of orthodox Islam and examines the evidence for the Christian counterclaim, preparing you with strong apologetic answers. This revised edition contains more resources and updated information throughout."

Genesis: "The Bottom Strip" of the Christian Faith, DVD, by Carl Kerby (Answers in Genesis)

From the publisher: "One of the world's most popular creation speakers, Carl Kerby uses creationism to explain the foundations found in Genesis, holding up the Bible's first book as critically important to doctrine and our everyday lives."

Genesis: The Key to Reclaiming the Culture, DVD, by Ken Ham (Answers in Genesis)

From the publisher: "Ken Ham's best-selling talk on the relevance of Genesis. A fast-paced DVD, it explains why belief in a literal Genesis is so important."

Lifeviews: Make a Christian Impact on Culture and Society, by R.C. Sproul (Revell, 1986)

A comprehensive book on world views. This book helps you understand how Christianity stands in contrast to different world views. It's like reading the opposing team's game plan.

So What's the Difference? by Fritz Ridenour (Regal Books, 1967)

This is a very helpful book in evaluating the differences between the major religions. It is common for professors to try to equate all religions as being the same or to say that all followers of religion worship the same God. It's important to know what makes Christianity different from the others.

The Universe Next Door, by James Sire (InterVarsity, 1997)

From the publisher: "When *The Universe Next Door* was first introduced more than 20 years ago, it set the standard for a clear, readable introduction to world views. In concise, easily understood prose, James W. Sire explained the basics of theism, deism, naturalism, nihilism, existentialism, Eastern monism, and the new consciousness.

"The second edition was updated and expanded to include sections on Marxism and secular humanism, as well as a completely reworked chapter on what is now widely known as New Age philosophy rather than new consciousness. Now the third edition offers further updating and revisions throughout, including a thoroughly revised chapter on New Age philosophy and, perhaps most importantly, a new chapter on postmodernism.

"*The Universe Next Door* has been translated into several languages and has been used as a text at over one hundred colleges and universities in courses ranging from apologetics and world religions to history and English literature. With the publication of the third edition, this book will continue to aid students, teachers, and anyone who wants to understand the variety of world views that compete with Christianity for the allegiance of our minds and hearts."

Understanding the Times: The Religious Worldviews of Our Day and the Search for Truth, by David A. Noebel (Harvest House, 1994)

This comprehensive and helpful book on world views is written by David A. Noebel, president of Summit Ministries in Manitou Springs, Colorado.

PARA-CHURCH GROUPS ON CAMPUS

Ambassadors for Christ — www.afcinc.org

Ambassadors for Christ Inc. describes itself as "a Chinese Christian mission to reach Chinese students and professionals in the United States and other parts of the world for Christ." Established and incorporated in 1963 in Washington, D.C., the headquarters remained there until 1974, when it moved to Paradise, Pennsylvania. AFC has regional staff at local university campuses involved in personal evangelism and discipleship, through Bible study groups, conferences, and seminars.

AFC Mission Statement: "AFC is called by God, in cooperation with local churches, to evangelize and disciple Chinese students and professionals in the US and other parts of the world, to motivate and equip them to impact the culture for the Lord; to mobilize and channel them into the service of Christ as a vital force for God's Kingdom."

Campus Crusade — www.ccci.org

Campus Crusade for Christ International's mission statement says the CCC "is an interdenominational ministry committed to helping take the gospel of Jesus Christ to all nations. We cooperate with millions of Christians from churches of many denominations and hundreds of other Christian organizations around the world to help Christians grow in their faith and share the Gospel message with their fellow countrymen."

Chi-alpha — www.Chialpha.com

Chi Alpha describes themselves as a "movement of college students earnestly following Jesus" with a presence on 200 college campuses. The Greek letters Chi (x) and Alpha (a) are the initials of a phrase written by the apostle Paul in the Bible. Translated, it means "Christ's sent ones." Chi Alpha meets on campus in all sorts of settings and sizes. Meetings are "informal, charged with music, given to humor, and deal with everything from relationships to the nature of truth. The goals of these gatherings are to meet with God, meet among friends, and meet real needs. Chi Alpha says they "work hard to learn from and join with international students. We strive to be multicultural. We see that faith and thinking are related."

InterVarsity Christian Fellowship — www.intervarsity.org

InterVarsity Christian Fellowship describes itself as "an evangelical campus mission serving more than 35,000 students and faculty on more than 560 college and university campuses nationwide. Incorporated in 1941, InterVarsity has a rich tradition of campus witness, thoughtful discipleship, and a concern for world missions."

In 2002–2003, InterVarsity had 810 undergraduate chapters on 565 campuses. Some campuses have separate outreaches to international students, sororities and fraternities, and ethnic minority groups. During the 2002–2003 school year, over 32,000 students were actively involved in InterVarsity chapters; 865 field staff supports these student groups. The next Inter-Varsity Urbana conference will be in 2006 at the University of Illinois.

The Navigators — www.navigators.org

Navigators describes themselves as helping "Christ's followers 'navigate' spiritually, coming alongside to support them as they search the Word of God to chart the course of their lives. The hallmarks of our ministry are one-to-one relationships and small-group studies focused on discipleship."

College campuses are just one of the settings where Navigators has staff. They also have staff on military bases in the inner cities, prisons, and youth camps.

Reformed University Fellowship — www.ruf.org

Reformed University Fellowship has a presence on 76 campuses across the United States. RUF is a ministry of the Presbyterian Church in America. RUF states that they bring to the campus "a heart for God, a love for the campus, and convictions that are well formed, deeply held, and which allow us to bring a fully orbed ministry to students. As a ministry of the Presbyterian Church in America, we reflect the historic positions of the Church which include: The full authority, inspiration, and inerrancy of the Bible, the necessity of new life in Jesus Christ, and the task of the Church to be the 'gathering and perfecting of the saints.' "

ASSORTED RESOURCES

Summit Ministries

Summit Ministries mission statement: Training servant leaders in world view analysis, equipping them to champion the Christian faith, inspiring them to love God with their hearts and minds.

Summit offers a variety of conferences, some lasting for a weekend, others for a week. Summit is best known for challenging two-week sessions located in Colorado or Tennessee. "The program combines 'intense class-room training with a youth camp atmosphere, peppered with time for sports and relaxation, informal discussions, small groups, local tours and worship. Students are equipped with a deep understanding of the Christian world view and an insightful grasp of the key issues of our day.'

"A typical Summit day includes morning classes and an afternoon filled with sports, free time, community service projects, or tours. Evening sessions include music and sharing, specially selected videos, and in-depth world view teaching.

"Each Summit student is part of a small group led by the Summit staff, providing opportunity for personal reflection and interaction. Iron sharpens iron as Christians challenge Christians to new heights of service and devotion."

Summit graduates rave about the experience and how practical the information is in the college classroom. For info go to www. summit.org.

Worldview Academy

Worldview Academy is the group that runs the magazine ads like the one with a male student's picture and copy that says, "Your son's GPA is 3.95, he got a 1350 on the SAT, and he ranks 3rd in his class. Is he ready to face Dr. Wells? He's not mean; in fact, he's the most popular guy on campus. Dr. Wells makes a game out of trivializing everything your son believes. He's good at it. He gets most students by asking why they think Christianity is true."

Worldview Academy has the picture. They also have a response. Their leadership camps train students ages 13 and up in world views, servant leadership, apologetics, and evangelism. "We know the challenges your student faces in our world today: a popular culture that encourages selfishness and mediocrity, an education system based on atheistic or New Age assumptions, and leaders driven by the desire for power and personal gain. Who can stand firm at such a time? Only the Christian who courageously pursues a deeper relationship with Christ, learning to think His thoughts and follow Him. Worldview Academy Leadership Camps challenge Christian students to 'prepare [their] minds for action' so that they can lead by serving with integrity."

Camps are hosted at a variety of locations through the country. For info go to www.worldview.org or call 800-241-1123.

About the Author

Abby Nye Suddarth is already making her mark as a talented young contemporary Christian author. During her college career she wrote *Fish out of Water — Surviving and Thriving as a Christian on a Secular Campus.* Taking fresh classroom experiences and insight born of her own struggle to adapt in a world of liberal academia often hostile to Christian worldviews, Abby sheds important light on the minefield of ideology and intolerance Christians can face at secular colleges. Providing important strategies and advice on becoming a successful Christian student in hostile academic waters, Abby creates a compelling safety net of information which can help others to not only survive, but to thrive in the classroom and in the college social scene. Positive, empowered, and standing on faith, Abby proves Christian students need not suffer in silence or abandon their faith in the ivy-covered halls of secular universities.

Today Abby is married with twin daughters. Her husband completed five years in the Army serving in Iraq, and has now transitioned to civilian work. They currently live in New Jersey where Abby has put her career as a physician assistant on hold to raise her girls. She is enjoying the adventures of being a stay at home mom!